Happiness To you

dear my love

and Martin Din

The End Was But A Beginning

A True Story

Raymond J. Castellani

www.raymondjcastellani.com

First published by Dog Ear Publishing
4010 W. 86th Street, Ste H
Indianapolis, IN 46268
www.dogearpublishing.net

ISBN: 978-159858-831-6
WGAW: 1281275

This book is printed on acid-free paper.

Printed in the United States of America

This book is dedicated to the fulfillment of Principles for the betterment of mankind – to enhance and to propagate ideals that have withstood the journey of the ages since the inception of humanity's birth –

CONTENTS

A TRUE STORY

I was four – the year was 1937 – I was in an orphanage in New York – when I first arrived I saw so many children running around playing – to me there was no joy in seeing what was before me – I can't remember who dropped me off nor time of year it was – must have been late summer – I do remember most vividly the feeling of loneliness that consumed my being – 1937 was and is a long time ago – and a little boy of four was to embark on the first plateau of what was to last my entire life – that being an empty feeling inside my very soul – for on that day I cried - when whoever or whatever left me in that orphanage - I cried - I cried - I cried – the aloneness consumed my heart that day - never to leave – never to be forgotten - never to be exchanged for happiness or fulfillment – unknown to me at that time - the tears of that day will remain forever embedded in the consciousness of the days and years to come - never to be blanketed by self-delusion or self-pity – never to be used for manipulation in any form – I cried literally for over a week – sometimes huddled in a corner – just weeping – when the tears subsided - reality set in – here I was alone with a bunch of little kids most likely feeling the same way I was – I can't remember – I can't remember one kid's name from that three and one-half years I was to spend there – that night I went up to the top floor – I believe the third floor – there before me were fifteen or so little beds all made up – and about ten or twelve four and five year olds – one thing was most prevalent – there was not one sound from anyone – I was told to get into some pajamas that were given to me and get into bed – the woman's name that was in charge was Mary – I will never forget her or her name – she was a virago-type woman – she was the keeper of the ward – no one uttered a sound - it didn't take long for me to realize who was boss – we were all in bed – I started to weep – that lonely

lonely feeling – I don't even know what it was I longed for – even to this day – I can't even remember if I knew my mother at that time – or who I knew – and then a lady clothed in black with a white collar came into the room – of course I didn't know at the time that she was a Sister of some order – Sister Mary – I also will never forget her – she came to my bedside - held my hand – looked at me – and said it's going to be okay – I didn't understand – I couldn't tell her what I was feeling – I didn't know myself – I wept most quietly – there seemed to be a knowing awareness in her of how I felt – I said a little prayer – God help me – God be by my side – God I love you – help me please – I feel so bad inside – I wept and wept some more – it did not deter my quest for His presence – many times during the next few years I would pray – it made me feel warm inside each time I said a prayer - I had nothing else going for me – I would pray and weep my life away – how long that was to be I did not know – I think that Sister Mary along the way told me to pray to the Blessed Mother – so I did many times – I didn't know God that is for sure – and I didn't know the Blessed Mother or who she was – but in between the tears I prayed to Her – She became my warmth – in my solitude – in my despair – in my hopelessness – in some strange way each time I prayed to Her - a calm came over me – I was so helpless – as I remember back – I knew absolutely nothing – but I prayed any way – it was my secret as I went to sleep - my name by the way was Raymond Johnston – I was also a bed-wetter – in the morning at times my sheet was wet – Mary was there to wake us up – go to the bathroom – brush our teeth – etc. etc. – we went back to our room and made our beds – my sheets were still wet – I made my bed without a word – I don't know what came next – I guess I went to breakfast – but after breakfast we all met in this large rec room – sat around the perimeter – and in walked Kerbin - Sister Kerbin – she was big – most stern to say the least – her eyes were piercing – there was no smile in her being – no warmth to her whatsoever – everyone knew not to say a word – just be quiet – she ruled with an iron hand – this is year 2004 – I can't believe I remember all the details of what went on so long ago – as I looked around that morning there were young boys all ages – they all had that look in their eyes of despair – this was to be my life for the next three and one-half years – the days came – I remember little things that happened along the way such as the smell of urine as I drew close to the bathroom – looking into that big dormitory and seeing seventy or so beds made up with a foot-locker beside each – in a year or so I would be moved to this area – I remember going to eat – many times Sister Kerbin would force food down me – one meal - liver was the meat of the day – it was forced down my throat – I remember it all came up – it didn't stop - they kept shoving the liver down – I kept throwing it back up – one thing I also remember - I never cried when these sort of things went on – one time we were gathered in that rec room – one of the boys tried to run away - he was caught – we all sat around the perimeter - a long table was in the center – the boy must have been fifteen years old – they - Mary and Sister Kerbin – stretched the boy out on the table - with a stick whipped and beat that boy –Sister Kerbin turned to us all and said - anyone who tries to run away from here will get the same - she turned and continued to whip that boy – when she was through the boy got off the table - in the most jerky movement - he just kept jumping up and down – myself and the boy sitting next to me snick-ered at the movement of the boy that just got beat – we did not real-ize the pain that accompanied the movement – Sister Kerbin came over to us – picked us up like kittens from the back of the neck and dropped us – she told us never to snicker again – the little boy next to me cried – I didn't – they could beat me - force food down my throat – strap me - I would never cry – the empty lonely feelings inside of me would bring tears many times each day - torment to my soul – now - and for the existence of my life – winter set in – nothing ever changed – Halloween came - they dressed us up – I was a tiger I remember – I don't remember anything about that first Christmas – the New Year came 1938 - February came - I passed five years of age – it was a Sunday I believe – I had a visitor – Aunt Babe was her name – she was my aunt – as soon as I found out she was to come I began to cry – when I laid my eyes on her - I began to plead with her to take me with her when she was to leave – I remember it was snow-ing – we had a snow sleigh – took several trips up and down a small hill – I was crying and begging her to please take me with her – she kept saying – "Sonny I can't - I'm sorry" Sonny was my nickname – we went back to the rec room - she bought me a candy bar - from our in-house little store – it was just a closet - off a little room on the side of the rec hall – it was time for her to leave – I looked at her again – begged – please please take me with you – we went outside to her car - she got in – closed the door – I touched the car as it moved away – I kept up with it – it was snowing so very much - she could not go very fast – we came to the large hill that she was going down to get to the highway – the snow was hitting my face – the tears filled my eyes – we reached the bottom – this is where I had to let go – I stood there alone – the snow covering my face – the tears shedding - with no control – I had to walk up that hill - the blinding snow I remember so well - I do not remember the cold – I don't know how long it took me to reach the top of the hill or get back to the rec hall – when I reached the inside – I remember going to some room – I huddled myself in a corner – I was so alone – I stayed there 'til it was time to go to bed – I lay in the bed crying – Sister Mary came to my bed - held my hand – said nothing – I knew she knew something of how I felt – no one came to see me again – Spring came – Summer – Fall – Winter – they were all the same to me – they moved me down to the big dormitory right next to the bathroom - I could smell that smell – but I was still a bed-wetter – and when I wet the bed Sister Kerbin would be quick to point that out - in the morning - in front of all she would say "Raymond Johnston wet the bed last night"- my head lowered – but that's all - no tears – no remorse – none of the kids made fun of me – there is one name that comes to mind – Mahoney – the only thing I can remember about him was he was much older than I was – he told me never to try and run away – woods surrounded us – and I would be caught and whipped – I listened – I have no recollection of the next year – I turned six that February of 1939 – the only feelings I ever had were sadness - many nights crying myself to sleep – I often times wondered what it would be like to be somewhere else – but I didn't know where somewhere else was – I was hardened to my surroundings – no one came to visit me – most of us knew how to act – how to go to bed at night – when someone new came in we all helped out – Mary each night would take a belt from one of the boys – if there was any talking – the strap would do it's talking – fifty or sixty boys in one room and not a sound – as I said I passed six that February and when spring came – I was shipped off to a farm in up state New York – I remember the name of the people who ran the farm – Sutton – Mrs. Sutton – it was another sad day – being dropped off again by some unknown person - in some unknown place – I remember there were two or three of us kids dropped - off – I remember the house – the kitchen with a big black wood burning stove – an ice box – water that was pumped from a well – the barn – there was an outhouse – never saw one of them before – and in front of the house a big tree stump – I saw a chicken killed on that stump and run around without it's head – I cried in dismay – I had to eat that chicken – I drank milk - warm and bubbly - fresh from a cow – my chores in the morning around 5 a.m. were to bring four cows in from pasture – have them milked – not by me – I never did get the hang of milking – I sure tried – I loved to touch the cows – there was a great feeling of warmth – and strength – there were two calves also in the barn – they were wiry and most beautiful – when I had free time I would spend time in the barn talking to the calves – when the cows were milked I brought them back to pasture – came back to the barn - fed the chickens – I can still here the chirps they made when I fed them – I don't remember having breakfast – my next choir was the one I most disliked – as I said there was an out house which meant there were no bathrooms in the house – my chore now was to empty the bowls full of urine that were under the beds – take them to the out-house and empty them – it sounds simple – but here is what I remember – the smell of urine – going to the outhouse - dumping the urine into and over the wooden cutouts – looking down as it hit piles of human waste – I also was the one who dumped lime through the wooden cutouts – I still remember how sick I used to get each morning when this chore came up – it was most unpleasant – I remember having to pull weeds in the fields where our vegetables grew – once a week on a Saturday - was bath-time – the water was heated on the wood-burning stove in the kitchen – there was a big wooden tub where the hot water was poured – I was embarrassed to get in the tub naked – so they put a small bathing suit on me so I could take a bath

– the weeks passed – August was here - now came the time when the fields of grass were to be cut for hay - first the grass was cut – laid in the August sun to dry – then raked into long mounds – then into big mounds every thirty feet or so – at the end of August we piled the hay which it was now - we had two horses that pulled the hay wagon – I remember lifting the pitchfork of hay into the wagon – when the wagon was piled high we brought it to the barn – there from a hoist pulley into the loft to be stored for winter – it amazes me that I can remember all the details of this summer from so long ago – I never smiled – I never went to the movie show – which were silent pictures I only saw at the orphanage – loneliness followed me - each day – each night – summer was over - back to the orphanage – the memory of being on the farm was pleasant except for that one morning chore – I can still feel the power of those cows and calves – I also remember a black bull that was on the farm – I never got too close but I did feel his strength from a distance – I saw for the first time a mother breast-feeding her newborn child – I sure did know what work was all about – the same routine followed as the previous years – school was and is a haze to me – I was approaching seven years of age - I couldn't read or spell – that I remember – I do not remember even being in school – the gray days of winter were here again -1940 – on a Sunday in mid winter I had a visitor - my mother – how sad it was for me and how I do remember – I cried at first sight when I saw her – started to beg and plead with her to take me with her - to no avail – she spoke softly to me as I wept – she said this was going to be the last year I was going to spend here – it didn't move me in any way – now was the time that meant something to me – a day was a year to my life – I could not conceive anything beyond the moments of the moment – I don't know how long we spoke – the tears just kept coming – she had to leave – I remember me running down that hill again as I ran down for my aunt Babe – I cried all the way down – the car disappeared – I stood there – alone – how alone I was – I can still feel the winter cold as I commenced my walk up the hill – I use to pray to God in my little way – I did get much solace – I felt a calm come over me each time I said a prayer – I didn't ask for anything – It just felt good to feel something outside of myself that warmed my being – I prayed that day – I got back to the rec room - the sadness and loneliness to this day I can still feel – I must have cried for days afterward – many times at night before I went to sleep I would weep – I don't think I can remember too much more about these three and one-half years – this was now the summer of 1940 on the farm again – same chores – same outhouse – same cows – chickens – the calves were cows – etc. - the same loneliness – the memory of these years are with me today - most fresh – the end of summer came – my mother came to the farm and picked me up – I was elated to see her – we spoke in the car – she said that I was not going back to the orphanage in New York – in my little mind at seven and one-half – a dream had come true – in a flash – no more being lonely – no more weeping – no more straps to go to bed with – no more boys getting whipped for running away – no more food being shoved down my mouth - no more dark days of winter – I have no memory of school in this time slot - yet I can remember the smell from the dormitory - and the urine from the bathroom – I can remember the corner of the room where I sat and cried for days on end – I do remember watching Charlie Chaplin in a silent movie but never a smile – I felt most good that day – I didn't know where I was going nor where I was going to live – as we were driving she told me she was going to marry a man named Jack Mayo – he was going to meet us at our destination in Troy, New York – I didn't quite know what was going to come about – I did know something not good was going to happen – as we drove into the city of Troy - drove up to an orphanage where Jack Mayo was waiting – my heart and my whole being was gripped with pain – the pain of loneliness consumed me - one more time - not a word came from my mouth – I could not believe what was happening – the vision of the three and one-half years in New York was – as it is today – most vivid – the situation most incredulous – I could not fathom what I was to do – I remember standing in front of a man that was in charge behind his desk - my head was down – my mother sitting on one side - Jack Mayo on the other – he introduced himself - asked me my name – I said Raymond Johnston – he acknowledged – he said that I was going to be staying here in this orphanage – to this day the words that came out of my mouth I will never forget – I looked at him straight and said "I will run away" - at which time he said "We will catch you" – I said "I'll run away again" – at that time he told my mother to take me in the hall to explain the situation to me – my mother told me that I had to stay - I had no place to run to – I looked at her as I looked at that man and said "I will run away" – we went back in the office I said nothing – I was left there crying on the outside - ever so alone standing in my own being – where was I to run to – where was I to seek refuge – I have no recollection of even having a meal at this orphanage – but this is what happened – I must have picked up some information that Troy was near Albany, New York – I am seven and one half years old now - trying to remember back - before I was put in that orphanage in New York – I knew my grandfather carried me in his arms when I was ever–so-young – I could feel that love somehow – I remembered he lived in Albany – but where – how far was Albany from Troy – how could I get there – someone told me there was a river separating Troy from Albany – was this true - I did not know – there was only one thought running through my head – how to run away - how to get to my grandfather – I was in the middle of nowhere – I didn't talk to anyone – I kept saying to myself " how am I ever going to get out of here"- this is what I remember - there was a river – the Hudson River – separating Troy from Albany – somehow I got information that piano lessons were given in Albany on each Saturday – I thought to myself - that could get me across the river to Albany but then what – I will be in a middle of a city not knowing where to go – in fact not knowing anything – completely devoid of any thoughts of how to even make a move in any direction whatsoever – I had to take a chance – going nowhere at seven and one-half years old did not enter my mind – fear never entered in – I knew I was going to run away from this orphanage - so I signed up for the piano lessons – I still can't believe how I can remember these facts from so long ago – and yet I can't remember a boy or girl's name – or what I ate – or where I slept – or anyone's face – or going to school - Saturday came – I remember getting into a station wagon – the drive seemed so long – we crossed the Hudson River over a long bridge it seemed – I don't remember much of the drive or any of the landmarks – what I was to do I did not know – an empty space comes into my head when looking back on this ride to the piano lesson – I just kept thinking I had to run away – but how was I going to get to my grandfather's – what comes to my mind at this time is this – the station wagon was traveling up a street called New Scotland Avenue – I passed an area that seemed somewhat familiar to me – I only had a few seconds for the recollection – a picture came to me of my Godfather Patsy Tyrone who was a member of the Black Hand – the forerunner of the Mafia – I loved him very much also – had not seen him in over four years – the picture that came to me in that moment was me running into a stucco wall – Patsy taking out a white handkerchief and holding it to my head to stop the bleeding – the moment flashed – I knew for some reason I was in familiar territory – as the station wagon proceeded up New Scotland Avenue - on the corner of a street that is called South Main Avenue I recognized the corner house – to this day it is the biggest miracle of my life – this was a convalescent home that belonged to my grand-mother – my grandfather lived there - in the cellar - that was made over into living quarters – he was a master builder of beautiful homes that stand to this day - what sight to behold as the station wagon passed by – he was there – I could feel him – my mind raced – what do I do – how can I get to him – I had nothing – no money – no phone number – I had the clothes on my back – I marked where that street and house were in my mind – I kept saying don't forget New Scotland Avenue – over and over as the wagon drove on – the station wagon never made a turn for about three or four miles up New Scotland and then it took a left turn into a convent – my mind knew exactly where I was in relation to where my grandfather lived – I don't remember taking any piano lessons or even sitting down at the piano that day or any other day – this is what I remember from sixty-two and one half years ago – I left the convent – the station wagon drove down New Scotland Avenue the same way it came up – as I passed New Scot-land and Main I saw the convalescent home again – my mind started to ponder – how could I get to the that house on New Scotland – as we drove through Albany – then across the Hudson River - I just kept trying to put some plan together – to no avail – back to the orphan-age – I don't remember anything that happened during that week – I don't remember any dormitory – any eating place – how the building looked – cold - warm etc. – just that mental image of the first moment I set foot in the office - when I told that man - my mother - that I would run away - them saying I would be caught – I do remember very vividly what happened to the ones that ran away and got caught in New York – not good – I do remember that episode really well – what was I to do – I took that trip to Albany the next Saturday – across the river - through Albany – up New Scotland Avenue – approaching Main Avenue – my heart beat ever so fast – here I was again so close – I felt my grandfather one more time – turned into that driveway for that piano lesson that I cannot remember taking – how strange – again leaving that convent – same route – through Albany – same river – same orphanage – same sick feeling inside – loneliness – tears that never stopped – no faces – no entities whatsoever – I had to figure some way to escape – but how – during this third week something came to me – a plan – this is what happened – Saturday came - off to the piano lesson I went – as the station wagon drove up New Scotland – I began to shake a little – for I knew I was going to make the escape – I had been one week thinking about this simple plan – will it work – I sure hope so – we turned into that driveway to the entrance of the convent – as I remember three of us at least got out of the wagon – through the doors – one person went into the piano lesson room - me and a boy my age sat on a bench outside the room – at this moment my heart was coming out of my chest – this was my plan – I leaned over to the boy next to me and said – "I am going to run away – when they come out and ask where I am – tell them you do not know where I am" – he told me that they would catch me and beat me – I said "They will not catch me" – I got up most slowly – walked to the door and out I went – I could run very fast even at seven and one-half – down that driveway onto New Scotland Avenue – I can still feel the wind in my face – looking behind me as I ran wondering if they found out that I had run away – my little plan was working perfectly so far – it all came together - I still can't believe what happened to this day – I felt the freedom of not being in that orphanage ever so briefly – so many things racing through my mind as I kept on running toward where my grandfather lived – is he going to be there – I knew the way into the house down stairs to the cellar - but is he going to be there – I kept on running – I started to cry for some reason – my life as it was came before me – my mother - my father who I didn't know – my Aunt Babe – the loneliness – the tears shed over the past four years – this plan of escape – will it work – I kept running – please be there Grandpa I kept saying as I approached that convalescent home – please be there – I ran as quickly as I could through the front door – through the hallway – around the stairwell down to the cellar – down the stairs I went – double doors faced me – I tried the knob on the right – it was locked – I went to my knees and started pleading – "Grandpa Grandpa please open the door" – I was so afraid the people from the orphanage would catch me – I was so full of tears – "Grandpa please - please - open the door"- then - what seemed like a long moment of my life – the key turned - the door opened – there stood my grandfather – a sight I so remember to this day – a moment of my life that has been - will always be a treasure beyond reproach – that moment my grandfather leaned down and picked me up – held me in his arms ever so gently – as I kept saying "Please Grandpa don't let them take me back – please – please – Grandpa"- these are the words he said to me that Saturday morning as he held me in his arms – " Nobody is going to take you anywhere anymore Sonny"- I put my head on his neck and wept – I felt safe for the first time in my short life – my grandfather stood six feet two inches tall and weighed around two hundred pounds – powerful body – large hands – spoke in broken English – he comforted my pain – he was the man who gave me my nickname of Sonny - after the song Sonny Boy by Al Jolson – when the song came out in the early Thirties after I was born - he said that he had a Sonny Boy – the nickname stayed with me for my life – I told him what I had done – that I had run away - the plan that I had to come to him – what was going to come next - I did not know – we walked up stairs – my hand in his – I did not let go – I remember we confronted my grandmother – she was aghast to say the least – when she said that I had to go back – my heart beat very fast – my grandfather spoke most soberly and said "Nobody is going to take Sonny anymore - he is going to stay with me"- I remember my grandmother saying to me as the police came to the front door to hide under the bed in the front room – I did so – I remember the conversation she had at the door – the police asking if she knew where I was – she said no – "He is missing" the police said – my grandmother said " You better find him" in her broken English- I never did go back to the orphanage – I was to stay with my grandfather in the cellar for the next three years – this was the most beautiful period of my life – there were no more tears – no loneliness – I was with my grandfather day and night – on Sundays I was with my Godfather Patsy of the Black Hand – I will go into detail about my godfather a little later – my grandfather put up a youth bed next to his big double bed – there was a nightstand with a radio and a clock – here is what we listened to for years – Jack Benny – The Great Gildersleeve – Amos and Andy – Fibber McGee and Molly – Duffy's Tavern – the Baby Snooks show – as I got older Inner Sanctum Mysteries – with the squeaky door – The Lone Ranger – these are some of the shows I remember – at night he would get me up so as not to wet the bed – and I didn't – we would eat together – any of the food I didn't like – he would quietly take it from my plate - eat it himself – we would shop at the Italian store together – I would hold his hand ever so tight – wherever we went – we would go to the lumber yard together – I would go on the jobs with him – he taught me how to use a hammer – chisel – saw – tools of his trade that he was so good at – Pete Fuscaleti – a man that he worked with I remember – we would come home – my grandmother would make an eggnog – put a little sherry in – I really liked the sherry in the eggnog – we would have supper – then to the cellar – please remember that the cellar was a living quarter – we would listen to our radio programs – how beautiful it was – Sunday would come around – my grandfather would let me go with my Godfather Patsy – he drove me to him each Sunday – he would pick me up after Patsy and I had dinner – either at Chipo's or Rocko Benonoplis' – the best Italian food I ever ate to this day – we ate in a private booth with closed curtain – all of the people belonged to the Black Hand – I learned not to ask any questions – my grandfather taught me that early on – for he confided in me that he built secret bootleg cellars for a guy named Podullo during Prohibition days – Patsy could be trusted – those dinners were so great – I was allowed to have a little wine with Seven Up – once in a while I would have a little too much – the people would say Sonny is a little umbreago – which means a little drunk - all week long I was with my grandfather – Sunday I was with my godfather – my godfather was teaching me understanding and love – he was most patient with me – in the summer he would take me to baseball games – my memory sort of wanders here – things coming into my head a little too fast – he had a beauty parlor that was a front for taking numbers – during those summer months I spent a few days with him – learned how to take numbers over the phone – code for name – how much – box it – which means if the number was 987 boxed would be 789 – so many years have passed and yet I remember so much – at night that good Italian food – my grandfather would pick me up – I had the best life – the Black Hand people loved me – my godfather loved me – my grandfather was my life – I learned how to do so much on my own – my instincts were most acute – my awareness of what to do - what not to do – most keen – where to go - where not to go – ever so present – who to speak to - who not to speak to – foremost – I was eight and one half soon to be nine – what happened now I still can't believe – my mother came back into the picture – she was to ship me off to her sister who lived in Syracuse – this happened once before – I just recalled – only it was my Aunt Babe in Yonkers – I stayed a few months with her – she is the one who came to visit me in that first orphanage – I don't know the time line on it – I do know that she and her husband - my uncle Earl - wanted to adopt me at the time – my mother said no – this time I remember very well – how happy I was these past years – what replaced that happiness – the tears came – coupled with that lonely feeling inside me – I was older now - the feelings were most pronounced – my mother drove me to Syracuse one hundred and fifty miles away from my grandfather – I don't remember any of the conversation at all – this is what I remember about my stay in Syracuse – this is my first recollection of going to school – I couldn't read – I couldn't spell – I was held back one grade already – I hadn't reached the third grade yet – Aunt Connie and Uncle Jack – cold was the winter – World War II was on – I collected tin cans for pennies – went to a Soap Box Derby - sold Cokes at the Derby to make money – I made money in the wintertime by shoveling snow off people's sidewalks - I also wet the bed again – no more radio – I cried myself to sleep almost every night – I was so unhappy – looking back on it now – I don't think I ever smiled - I found out that my mother had married that man Jack Mayo – I flunked the second grade – I had to somehow get back to my grandfather – Syracuse was not the place for me – my aunt and uncle knew it - after nine months back to Albany I went – I stayed with my grandfather one more time – listened to that radio – saw my godfather come Sunday - now I took the bus alone to downtown Albany – went to the picture shows by myself – had those beautiful Italian dinners at Rocko's or at Chipolo's – drank my wine with Seven Up - got a little umbreago – I used to see John Wayne in those Marine Corps movies – The Sands of Iwo Jima – what an impression it always made on me – my grandfather was working on a new nursing home in Schenectady that my mother was to run – I went to work with him each day – we drove to Schenectady each morning from Albany - it was about fifteen miles or so - in his Franklin car – I remember it had a rumble seat I used to sit in – I love my grandfather so very much – even to this day – the new nursing home in Schenectady on Union Street was going to be my new home – I was to see my grandfather several times each week and my godfather come Sunday – but I must sleep at the nursing home each night come fall – it was the best I could do – I made my first friend – his name was Joe Kime – there are so many things I remember in this portion of my life – I was left alone most every day this summer to run the streets – Joe and I would sneak into people's cellars - collect Coke bottles worth two cents – beer bottles worth five cents – I always had money – a movie was fourteen cents – a candy bar - five cents – a Coke also five cents – I don't ever remember asking anyone for money – I would go to Albany at night with my grandfather – back to Schenectady in the morning – meet Joe – off we would go – run run all day long – play – movies - candy – Cokes – I had no fear – I never thought the summer would end – but it did – as I write this now some sixty-four years later – sadness reflects inside me – during these summer months many times Joe and I would take our money - off to a double feature we would go – this is where I would much learn much about things happening in the world – between features a cartoon - then a newsreel – I remember so well a horse that would run and win – never the favorite – it had a red saddle – a red bridle – and wore blinkers – it was the first and only toy I ever had as a kid – I bought a lead horse in the five and dime store – it was about two inches tall – two inches long – about half inch thick – weighed about an ounce - it had the red saddle – bridle and blinkers – I can still feel that little toy in my hand – I had it for a long time – every time Joe and I would go to the movies sure enough the horse was running in the newsreel – and won – I felt a closeness with that horse – I slept with it – it was always in my pocket – I would derive strength from it – the horse's name was Seabiscuit – many times I would see the horror of the bodies being thrown into the mass graves from the death camps – they flopped as they were being thrown – I will always have that picture in my head – I will always remember the look of death on the faces of the people behind the barbed wire – I was so young - but I felt so much – Joe and I would spend time in the school playground each day – we would play marbles – I would win many marbles from the boys in the school yard – my pockets would be full at the end of each day – how beautiful everything was – I had my grandfather – my godfather – and a best friend named Joe – and of course my horse Seabiscuit – remembering back to the summer of 1942 or thereabouts – I could run like a deer – I could fight – wrestle – all athletic events – I was gifted as far as having a wonderful agile body – each night I would go home with my grandfather – have our dinner – I was allowed to have a small glass of red wine – we would go to the cellar – I would take a bath – then off to bed - we would listen to Fibber McGee and Molly – I can still here my grandfather laugh – wake up the next day and repeat it all over again – of course come Sunday - I spent with my Godfather Patsy – sometimes we would go to see the Albany Senators baseball team play – a class A league – I remember the player manager's name Pinky May – I can still see me walking down Pearl Street toward the center of town with my Godfather surrounded by five or six members of the Black Hand – we walked slowly – all speaking Italian – with their straw hats – canes – spats – dressed so beautifully – diamond-studded cufflinks and tie clasps – we would go to Chipo's or Rock Benonopoly's for dinner – I remember the dinners so well – I would get a little umbreago – I would go back to my grandfather – Monday was soon here – it amazes me what I remember – the feelings that come over me as each reflection passes in view – I relived this summer many times as the years came forth – I had nothing - yet I had everything – the years in that orphanage in New York were and will be a reminder of how things could be – I never spoke to anyone about my tenure there – I never knew what the future was going to hold for me – I had a great awareness even at this young age – even though I could not read or spell at this age – I was to stay in Schenectady this coming year at the nursing home on the third floor - fall was here – I believe I was in the fourth grade – the only remembrance I have of this school is me standing in front of the class - as the teacher had told me – minutes before I had asked to go to the bathroom – she made me stand in front of the class until I wet my pants in front of the whole class – I remember the puddle at my feet – it was demoralizing – I took off running out of the classroom – hit the street and started walking back to the nursing home – it was a long walk – it never had a lasting effect on me – for some reason – I don't think I ever wet again – self or bed – I was getting on in years - almost nine come February – I don't remember anything else from that school – I do remember going to another school in a month or so – do not remember any lessons whatsoever – the nursing home was a different story – I remember the smell of urine most of all – I remember seeing the sick – breathing heavy – gasping for breath – I remember the moans of the dying – these are not pretty pictures – even to this day – the patients would come in to the nursing home - but would die there – they had lived their lives – all walks of people came in – every time - throughout my life - when the words nursing home came up - or I would pass a nursing home – I felt a lonely feeling come over me – the same feeling I had in that orphanage – emptiness – the prevailing - most prevalent feeling - that will be born to me at this young age of eight - is and was the cornerstone of my make up – these eight years were filled with emotions that I came to rely on in future years of my life – I knew pain – I knew loneliness – I had understanding in my limited fashion of others – I was able to feel another's sadness – I was able to say a small prayer to God - have that warm feeling come over me – not knowing why – I knew what crying was all about – that feeling in the lowest part of my stomach – the hurt – the hurt – the hurt – I knew what death was – I had seen it so many times – I knew what the agony of death was also – how many times was I a witness – I knew the power of love - when my grandfather picked me up in his arms – I also felt the power of a man that loved me – I could be picked up by the nape of my neck and never cry – someone come to visit me in that orphanage I would cry for days – the paradoxes of life were in place – as I stated - I do not remember any classes whatsoever in school – I remember walking to school in the winter – how cold it was – Christmas came – I do not remember any presents – I do remember a Christmas tree however – there was no radio on the third floor – no grandfather to be with to listen to our programs – I would stay with him on weekends – and be with my godfather on Sundays – my mind would wander at this young age – I was always dreaming – places I've never been – things I've never seen – I do remember most vividly making a scrapbook of a football player named Tommy Harmon – I believe he played for Michigan University – his number was 98 – he was an All-American – always played with a ripped jersey – in any sport magazine I could find - I looked for number 98 – I found many pictures – the scrapbook was complete – I guess my education was not going too well – that summer - back to Albany – South Main the nursing home my grandmother ran – I do not remember how many schools I went to in my first four years of learning - but I do remember I had to repeat two grades before the fifth grade – so here I was back in Albany with my grandfather - I loved it – with my godfather on Sundays – baseball games – taking numbers in the beauty parlor – taking that walk on Pearl Street – with those beautiful people all dressed up – straw hats – cane – spats – and diamond tie clasp – well as fate would have it – I was sent off to a summer camp – much to my dismay – the name of the camp was Tec–A –With-A – I guess the wisdom of my mother – her new husband – thought it best for me to be at camp with boys my own age – how wrong it was remembering back – our mattresses were filled

with straw – which went on wooden bunks in tents that we stayed in
– here I was again – alone – those feelings of emptiness came over
me – when they left – the tears came – I spent two most unhappy
weeks there – during that time I remember fighting a lot – with one
kid - they put boxing gloves on us – I beat him bad – I was always
getting in trouble for fighting – it was not a big deal as I remember –
my mind would always be with my grandfather – my godfather also
– I never did understand why I was away from the two people that I
loved so very much – I was just glad not to be back in that orphanage
– the year was 1943 – the War was still going on - it seemed I had
lived a lifetime – yet I was only ten – so many pictures come to me
of the past – so many memories – that boy getting whipped on that
table in the orphanage – Sister Kerbin picking me and my friend up
by the nape of the neck – me wetting the bed – the long walk up that
hill to the orphanage in the wind and snow – tears – tears – more
tears – after my Aunt Babe came to visit me – the great escape – how
I loved that moment with my grandfather when he picked me up in
his arms – the power of his love – the Sundays with my godfather –
the dinners with him and the members of the Black Hand – Syracuse
– Schenectady – that short moment in Troy when I told the head man
I was going to run away – the baseball games on Sunday – the summer with my friend Joe Kime – the horror of the death camps – the
U. S. Marines that died on the beaches – the ever present warm feeling that would always come over me when I said a prayer - the agility
I had to handle myself at all times – the insight I had to see trouble
when it came – the awareness of life itself – the knowing - the not
knowing - how I knew – I remember meeting my father twice before
I was ten - the vague recollection of being with him on a truck putting
red flags as road dividers on the highway after a white line was
painted - comes to mind for the very first time – the second time I
only remember him making me a snowman – it must have been in
Watertown, New York – I was so very young – these are only flashes
in my mind – prior to being put in the first orphanage – I think - the
third time he came to visit me at the nursing home – this time I
remember most well – we sat together in the office - he drew me a
peanut man – like on the Planters Peanut package – it was beautiful

– there was a great sadness that surrounded him – he spoke very softly – there was kindness in his eyes – there was a great gentleness that accompanied him - he said he was glad I was with my grandfather - this was the third time in my life - meeting with my father – he left – a part of me went with him – I knew so much of the love he had for me – I knew he was helpless in this situation – I can still feel the hurt of his soul – strange that this was my third time with him – few words were spoken – yet how much I remember – maybe he felt my sadness - as I felt his – we touched each other in a very profound way – for the memory of that day has never vanished - yet I did not know what grade I was in – I could not read – spell – or write – my grandmother bought a house down from the nursing – 380 New Scotland Avenue – my grandfather was to have a room on the third floor – I was to have my own room on the second floor – it was the first time in my life I had a room of my own – this was not a big deal – the time spent with my grandfather in the cellar at the nursing home will always be paramount – nonetheless here I was – my grandfather living upstairs – my godfather come Sundays – at a place that I believed I was going to stay for a while – the rest of the summer of 1943 - I was outside most of the time – I made my money by cutting lawns – finding beer and Coke bottles – made friends with the family next door – the Hansens - four boys and four girls – did a lot of playing on the streets that summer – August was coming to an end – which meant back to school – I remember a short stint in a Catholic school – about a month or so – but because I couldn't read and was so far behind in every subject – I guess my grandmother and the principal decided to take me out of that school - place me in another school called - The Albany Academy – a most prestigious educational institute – founded 1812 - the cost being I had to repeat the fourth grade – at the time I knew nothing – one more school in the long line of schools I went to – so here I was - ten going on eleven - in the fourth grade – I have absolutely no recollection of learning anything whatsoever in school at any time during these primary years – but this was my beginning - unknown to me at the time – Miss Swantee was my fourth grade teacher – she was most gentle with me – she knew I had a problem in my schoolwork – couldn't read spell and so on – I remember looking out the classroom window - seeing all the cadets lined up in formation in front of the school – never realizing some-day I would be standing there – the students were fine with me – I walked home each day – graham crackers and milk were my dinner many nights – when my grandmother would come home – I had my eggnog with my sherry wine – when my grandfather was home early – we had pasta - meatballs – bread – etc. - I was always allowed to have wine with supper – the relationship between my grandfather and grandmother was not good – when my grandfather and I lived in the cellar on Main Avenue the relationship was not noticeable – when the three of us were together – at the new home - different story – I used to tell her not to speak of my grandfather the way she did – it was poison to my ears – nonetheless that is the way it went – winter was here – I made my money shoveling driveways and sidewalks with Jim Hansen next door – we would get up at four in the morning – work until school time – sometimes skip school – we would make ten or twelve dollars a day – a lot of money – I bought a pair of ice-skates – learned how to skate on Washington Park Lake at night – would jump barrels – race – anything that had competition – during the winter this routine was duplicated many a day - my mind while in school would always be out the window – the teacher had to call me back from that gaze - I would come home from school – before I went outside I would pass the buffet that held this liqueur called anisette – it tasted like licorice– sure was good - and warmed me up to go outside – I would see my godfather every Sunday – had dinner at the restaurant – beautiful dinners – had my Seven Up and red wine –would get a little umbreago – and home I would go – I thought time stood still - I never realized how fast time would go by – spring was here – I passed my eleventh birthday that February eighteenth 1944 – the War was still going on – I had my bedroom on the second floor my grandfather had his room on the third floor – would have supper with him every night – listen to the radio programs each night – life seemed good – I always had that empty feeling inside – I would pon-der back through my previous years of my life – remembering those tear filled days and nights – how many places I have been – how many cities – but here I was eleven years old – living at 380 New

Scotland Avenue – with my grandfather – with my own room – I played hard – worked hard – did not like school – I thought it was a waste of time – I still couldn't read or spell – made no difference to me whatsoever – I had my godfather on Sundays – dinner with the members of the Black Hand – I would get a little drunk – my week was complete – times during the week I would go down to the wine cellar and drink from the wine vats – loved the red wine – when it was good – sometimes it had turned into vinegar – not so good to drink – school was over – I made it into the fifth grade - summer was starting – I was alone most every day – made my money by working on a farm – Wally's Farm - it was called – I got fifty cents a bushel for string beans – made two dollars in the morning – two dollars in the afternoon – hard work – played hard - played 'til the late hours – roller skating – stickball – baseball – basketball – again anything that was competitive – during many weekdays I would go down to my godfather's beauty parlor – spend most of the day with him – take numbers over the phone – have milkshakes – go to the movies – he always gave me silver dollars – we would go to Chipo's for dinner – everything was most beautiful – I would take the bus back to 380 - see my grandfather - then to bed – one evening that summer I was having dinner with my godfather with my mother – just the three of us – I noticed my Godfather Patsy was having trouble eating – his fork fell to his plate – he had trouble talking – he motioned to my mother also to myself - that he was okay – my insides knew something was wrong – I can still see him to this day - what a beautiful man he was – he died that night of a stroke – part of me fell - when I heard the news – to this day I have never forgotten my Godfather Patsy – he held me in his arms when I was so very young – he stopped the flow of blood from my forehead when I ran into a stucco wall – I remember so well with his white handkerchief – the beauty parlor – the dinners – the Sundays – with all the members from the Black Hand – the chocolate milkshakes – the silver dollars he gave me so freely – even the wine with the Seven Up – taking numbers in the beauty parlor – the movies I went to – the man that committed suicide and lay in his own blood – it happened minutes before we got to the site where the man lay motionless – my godfather gently moved me past the scene – explained to me how sad this was - how this man must have been so desperate – how much mental pain this man was in to do what he did – I can still see the picture of the man's head laying in his own blood surrounding his face – most of all I remember the compassion he had for me – the wisdom he transferred to me – he loved me with no conditions – how vivid a portrait – of kindness – gentility – of caring for a little boy – I cried – that same lonely feeling came into my being – the finality of death – this portion of my life with my godfather was over – but his teaching remain – my grandfather was my whole life now – we would go to work together – he taught me every use of every hand tool there was at the time – the power of his being I was beginning to feel - to sense – my grandmother for some reason disliked him with a passion – much to my dismay – she would castigate him behind his back to me – to poison my mind against him I guess – it never worked – each time I told her to stop – my world with him could not be shaken – the summer of 1944 was coming to an end – I played hard – I learned much – I worked hard – I cried much – the War was still going on – I also got my first two-wheeler cost three dollars – my grandfather paid for it – it was an old bike – my grandfather fixed it up – it was my bike – I loved it – I was getting ready to go back to school – the Albany Academy – I was to be in the fifth grade – still could not read or spell – did not have any interest in school whatsoever – my teacher's name this year was Miss Anderson – another kind person to me – most understanding – I would ride my bike to school each day – back to 380 – be with my grandfather – eat supper – and we would sharpen his tools for the next day – listen to a few radio programs then to bed – my Sundays without my godfather was a reality most difficult to digest – school was over one day – I was on my bike riding out of the school driveway – one of the school buses stopped in the middle of his left turn – I kept going – as I moved out beyond the stopped bus a car came at that split second – I was hit – thrown several feet to the grown – lay there – I reenacted the whole incident as I lay there – I made a move on my bike that was on the blind – truly my fault – I filed this episode in my mind to be used the rest of my life – I got up – the driver of the car was most shaken – I said I was okay – I looked at my bike – my beautiful bike that my grandfather put together for me – it was unrideable – I walked home with the bike – I cried - I felt so bad – not because I got hit by a car – not because my bike was all twisted up – but because my grandfather bought and made this old bicycle a treasure for me – the touch of his hands permeated the body of the bike – the learning process of life was always in progress – I could feel - touch – sense – the appeal of others – I could hear their cry of despair – although I never said anything – winter came – snow – shovel more sidewalks – skip a few more school classes – make a little more money – ice-skate on the lake in town – jump those barrels – come home late – start all over again the next day – many a Thursday evening my grandfather and myself – would go to a bakery in the Italian section of town at 8 p.m. sharp to get a piece of fresh pizza – Condelina's was the bakery – it was dough with a little red sauce – seasoning – no cheese – long before pizza became popular – it sure was good – February 18 1945 my birthday came – I now was twelve – my mother moved in to 380 that year I do not know where Jack Mayo was – my mother was a tortured soul – I remember her sitting in a chair in the living room having her coffee and smoking – that look on her face – so sad – I remember coming home one day and I had the smell of ether on me – I was with a friend of mine Ed MacDonald – his father was a doctor – we helped ourselves to some ether – poured some of the ether into an Alka-Seltzer glass tube bottle – which is what the Alka-Seltzer came in – put a handkerchief over the top and started to sniff the ether – just before we would pass out we would back off – a weird sensation – to say the least – the only trouble was the ether smell was with me when I came home that night – I could not explain what I did – nor who I was with – nor where I got the ether from – I knew from that day on I was not to go any where with the smell of ether on me – summer was here again - I did complete the fifth grade although I still could not read or spell – It was the first time I stayed in one school for two years straight - I guess this next little episode happened in mid summer – It was sometime in July - my aunt Connie got me ready to meet my father at the Albany railroad station downtown – I remember getting ready that morning – she was getting a good part in my hair – I looked at her -

asked her what should I call him – she said call him father – he is your father – this will be the fourth remembrance of him – I recalled each time – the red flags put down from the back of the moving truck for road dividers – the snow man he built for me – the peanut man he drew for me – now to meet him at the railroad station – I remember so vividly the ride down to the station – I must have been nervous – I do not remember any conversation my aunt and I had – we made the station – she let me out in front – I walked in – it was a big place – as I kept walking - my father met me – he took me by the hand – over to the benches – we sat – the sense of deep sorrow came through his being – I cannot remember any words we spoke – but the feelings generated in those few brief moments – I will never forget – the love he had for me – the compassion – the understanding – the monumental troubles he experienced in his life – the sorrow he felt for me in my life – he said he was sorry but never spoke a word – the look in his eyes – the despair he felt as a human being – the hopelessness he felt as a father – everything he wanted to be to me - but couldn't – a great feeling gripped me inside – the loneliness I felt – all those tears of despair for so many years I shed as a young boy – the emptiness in my soul – the moment came - ever so short – but it came – we were together – understanding each other on an unexplained level – again no words – just feelings – he gave me two dollars – put his arms around me – held me for a few moments – turned - walked down the ramp to the tunnel where the trains are – I ran this scene hundreds of times in my head through the years – but at that moment when he walked out of sight – the imagery that took place for a life time came into play - the feelings are so real – I walked with him – got on the train – I thought his thoughts – I looked out the window as the train left the station – tears were in his eyes – overpowering loneliness – destiny had prevailed – he was never to see his son again – he knew this as the train left the station – the unimaginable agony he felt – how vivid my imagination – how real the imagery of my memory – yet so real – that must have been one of the most lonely train rides ever taken – my learning process of life was again portrayed – World War II came to an end this year of 1945 – the atomic bomb was dropped on Hiroshima and Nagasaki - eighty thousand people plus were killed at each city – I remember seeing the bomb going off in the newsreels at the movie house – never did realize the destruction – the horror – the complexities of hate – that bomb caused – that day in August 1945 was to end all wars in the future – the atomic age was upon us - I reflected back when I first heard the news over the radio that Pearl Harbor was attacked in 1941 – the newsreels – Marines hitting the beaches – the dead bodies floating in the water – Auschwitz – Dachau - the death camps – the dead bodies thrown into the mass graves – so very limp they were – the faces of the living dead – these are images I have never forgotten – I still feel the horror of it all – man's inhumanity against mankind – I felt so much pain on behalf of all those souls – the fear that went through each as they were paraded into the camps – the wide eye stare each had – the bewilderment that formed each person – I felt the end as each was led into the chambers where the lethal gas was administered – the cries of despair – the smell that permeated the air of the cremations that followed – the cadaverous – emaciated – hollowed gaunt look that accompanied each – as they tried to live one more day – I was so very young – my feelings ran so deep – whenever I was alone so many of these feelings surfaced in my consciousness – I was always aware of my surrounding – I could sense another's aura in a split second – I knew what people were going to do before they knew – an extra sense so to say – I could visit any situation – I could intuitively know and see the picture at hand - the summer was fast-moving – I worked on the farm – made my four dollars a day – picked strawberries at five cents a quart – string beans at fifty cents a bushel - cut lawns – played hard 'til night came – fall came – back to school – Miss Ives was my sixth grade teacher – I was more interested in sports than I was in anything else – I played football in the sandlot after school – always back to 380 – there was an incident that happened one morning - at 380 - I will never forget – I heard some yelling inside the house from my aunt Babe – "I'm going to kill you Mother" - she yelled – as I came through the back door my grandmother grabbed me and put me in front of her as a shield – I looked up the three stairs to the kitchen door way and I saw Aunt Babe pointing a silver handgun at us – she kept yelling I'm going to kill you mother – my grandmother kept yelling – "You won't kill Sonny" – Babe kept it up – pointing that gun at us both – I backed my grandmother out the door with me in front of her – I did not know whether Aunt Babe was going to shoot or not – all I knew was to get out in the open spaces – all these moments I speak of - seemed so long – it all happened in about fifteen seconds – on the way out I remember not knowing if a bullet was going off – I never did talk about that incident ever – nonetheless 380 was my home – I would have endured anything to be with my grandfather - I helped my grandfather with the tools – sharpening – cleaning – etc. - I loved being with him – he was my life – I loved him so much – again I do not know what I learned in the sixth grade – except one day Miss Ives my teacher stood up in front of the class – flayed her arms as conducting a band and said "'Of' is always a preposition" she repeated it about ten times with her arms flaying – I did learn that "of" was always a preposition – never forgot it – I don't know when I got to use it much – but that's what I learned in the sixth grade – I still didn't know how to read or spell – but I did make it into the seventh grade – it was called the first form at the Albany Academy – this was to be in the fall – summer first - there was talk that my grandfather was going to build a home for me to live in with my mother and Jack Mayo – It became a reality the summer of 1946 – I was thirteen – my grandfather and I set out to build a house on Van Schoick Avenue in Albany – I remember putting the lines out to get the dimensions of the house and to dig the foundation – it was a one story three bedroom home – I was going to have my own room in my own home – what a concept – we worked all summer – again going back to 380 – cleaning the tools – sharpening the saws – chisels – etc. – I learned so much that summer – the intuitiveness of how to put things together – to work side by side with my grandfather – the knowledge he transmitted to me – I have forgotten – we ate our supper together – drank our wine – listened to the radio – got up early – went to Van Schoick – we did this all summer long – fall came and back to school – first form – we wore uniforms – I met some of my lifelong friends that fall – Al Meyer – Charlie Stone – Dick Beamish – these along with Prentiss Carnell – Ed McDonald – Jim Caird – Dick Hoyt – Duncan MacAffer – Heath Twichell – Irwin

Smith – Pat Crowe – Doug White - when I was in the fourth grade I looked out of my classroom window and saw the battalion forming each morning – now I was in formation – learning how to march – execute the manual of arms – dress right – etc. – we had different teachers for different classes – my English teacher was Mr. Fullaytor – I did not fool around in his class – I remember him well – most stern – well versed in the English language – a great command of verbal communication – it was getting hard for me to keep up with the studies – resorting to what was going to be a way of doing things for the next six years - I began to copy homework from the smarter boys in class – when tests came –I wrote the answers on my hand – small pieces of paper – sat next to my friend Al where I could see his test paper – most sophisticated – I just did not have time to study after school – the headmaster's name was Mr. Meislahan – six foot three or four – I mention him - for as the years passed – I would be sent to his office many times – stand before him to be reprimanded – that year I started to play organized football – basketball - baseball – swim – track – I could participate in all these sports – this is what I did in all my spare time on the streets – 'til all hours of the night – fall winter – summer spring – I would help my grandfather on Saturday – Sunday also – I was to turn fourteen that February – I can't remember how I got it – but that winter I got my hands on a pint of whisky – I hid it in my dresser drawer – would take nips from it each day – that along with the wine in the wine cellar – but the hard whisky sure was good – I do remember that every time I had my Seven Up with wine - with my Godfather Patsy – I always wanted a little more – so here I am at fourteen remembering how I drank the wine in the cellar from the vats – when it turned to vinegar - not so good - dinners always wine – anisette when it was cold – filling it up with water as I drank it – my eggnogs - always with sherry – I had muscatel – I became a connoisseur of red wine – I could tell it was good by the smell – but that whisky sure was a different glow – my grandfather and I worked on the new house all winter long – me on Saturdays and Sundays – my grandfather all during the week with Pete Fuscaletti a master carpenter – the house was looking most beautiful – I could not believe that I was going to have a home of my own to live in – I did notice my grandfather was a bit slow to move at times – I tried to be more helpful – picking up the tools every night – putting them away each night – it was spring of 1947 – time came fore me to go into the eighth grade and I made it – don't know how – still could not read too well for sure – nonetheless I was promoted – summer was here – helping my grandfather for sure – the house was going to be ready in the fall – I also started working in the bowling alleys – it took a while to break in – I used to go to the alleys three or four times a week looking to set pins – but each time I went they would not use me –the reason being – I was too young - did not have working papers – it did not stop me – I kept going back maybe ten times – then one Sunday afternoon – the bowling alley was in full swing – there I sat knowing I was the only pinsetter left – please understand – I never set pins in my life before – the man in charge at the desk looked at me and said – "You're up" my chance at last had come – down in the pits I went – most pinsetters were of the age group from eighteen to thirty or more – here I was fourteen – how it worked I only saw others doing it – so here I was – in the center of the pit was a foot lever - I was to put the front part of my right foot into the hole where the lever was and press down – at which time ten metal pegs rose up from the ally where the pins were to be placed – each pin had a hole in the center – I would place each pin on a metal peg and release the foot lever – now the bowler was ready to bowl – I was slow – which the bowlers did not like – that first day was not an easy time for me – I learned all there was to learn about scoring – strikes – spares – etc. from sitting – waiting to get the call – as time went on I learned how to jump alleys – hold two pins in each hand also hold my own with the older pinsetters – on my breaks I would eat French fries in the coffee shop – I made eight cents a line – plus tips – about fifty cents per – I would come home with my pockets bulging – maybe ten to fifteen dollars – I was still at 380 – fall was here – back to school – an incident happened that fall in the school yard – there was a boy surrounded in a wide circle being spit upon – I jumped in the center – told the group to spit on me – I was ready to fight each and every one – no one made a move – Charlie Stone came in the center with us also – the boy's name was Paul Golubb – he was a cripple – he had polio as a child –

my heart felt so much compassion for Paul – I thought about that incident many times – how he must have felt when it was happening – the fear – the aloneness he suffered – I never once made fun of – chided – belittled – or put out of context of life – any human that had a handicap of any sort – winter was here – my grandmother told me my grandfather was ill – the news devastated my very existence – I did not show any emotion in front of my grandmother – all the derogatory statements she – my mother – my Aunt Babe and the rest of the family made through the years – were now to be transformed into understanding – a lesson for me to learn for sure – a man my grandmother disliked for so many years - at this point of my grandfather's end – came - compassion – and love –incorporated in her being - I realized in this time period of my life – what a waste of time it was harboring such ill feelings toward one another – they had a whole life time to love him - but did not – instead gave him discord – torment – joyless days – the house he built for me took the last bit of strength he had – for this summer of 1948 he was to die – he died in my room - in my bed - at 380 New Scotland Avenue – I saw him take his last breath – I have never forgotten – I wept by myself – the loss ever so great – he had given me my life - when he picked me up in his arms - told me nobody was going to take me away anymore – he taught me how to smile – he comforted my soul – he gave me strength – he gave me courage – I can still feel his power – I reflected back to all the radio shows we heard together – how he would eat the food I did not like – how he was so gentle with me - how he was so patient with me – how we would work together on his jobs – the process of learning how to use the hand tools that built beautiful homes – he was – he is still my beacon of life – he has – will always be - in the present for me – never faded by time – I will meet him again – I am fifteen - summer will soon turn into fall - back to the Academy - yes I will start the ninth grade – unable to read or spell – most sophisticated on how to get by – there was a girl I met – her name was Linda Carnell – she was one of the most important single persons I had in my corner to get me through high school – she did all my book reports – read the books – wrote the compositions that had to be written – on and on – we learned how to dance together – I

remember Louis Armstrong's Give Me A Kiss To Build a Dream On
– La Vie en Rose – so many beautiful songs of the late forties – the
athletic ability that was given to me at such an early age was to come
into being – my fastest time in the sixty yard dash was made that
spring when I was still in the eighth grade – was 7.2 seconds – a great
achievement for a young boy – I played freshman football – basketball – swam on the swim team – baseball – and ran track – there was
nothing in the line of sports I could not participate in – a true gift –
of course there was still school to contend with - Alan Meyer still
gave me all his homework – he did not like doing it – but he did it
anyway – he was my dearest friend – we were inseparable – he -
Charlie Stone – myself – would travel the next four years through
high school together – I did find very soon that we all loved to drink
– so as the nightlife became a lure – Al – Charlie – myself – became
connoisseurs of just about every bar in Albany – Charlie was a magnificent athlete – Al was - but did not care – so as the years progressed – school always stayed the same – ninth grade became
history – that year in 1949 I passed my sixteenth birthday – was
going into the tenth grade the fall of 1949 – the summer was rich – I
worked for BT Babbit & Co. – the company made cleanser for pots
and pans – I made forty two dollars a week – worked eight hours a
day – five days a week – loading the cleanser into box cars – all day
long – when I got off – met Charlie and Al – off we would go to one
of many bars – I thought this time period would never end – I knew
just about everyone in the city from all schools – because Charlie an
I played sports – the nightlife was most terrific – we barhopped many
a night – I made a trip to New York City one weekend – I would like
to tell a little story about me in the big city – Fifty Second Street
between Seventh and Sixth was a most glorious section – here lies
some of the most historical jazz clubs in the world – the first club we
went into was most beautiful – the lights were low – the room was
about twenty feet wide - thirty five long – the aroma of drink permeated the air – it was smoked-filled – there was a small dance floor –
a jazz quintet powered the small room with elegant sounds – those
sounds rang so – I can still hear them – being a virtuoso at dancing -
so I thought – all my wisdom about life – again - so I thought – very

adept in the con game – I was in my element – there was a young girl about twenty-one or so – her name was Joan – she was some good-looking young woman – she sat down next to me – started talking – asked if I would buy her a drink – of course – we danced when the music was right – there I was in love again – I was drinking rye and ginger – why I remember I do not know – I thought to myself how can I be so lucky to meet a girl so great – we must have spent about three hours in this magnificent mode – could not get any better – I do not remember how many rounds of drinks we had - but quite a few – now came the moment of truth as I remember – I ordered another round for us – reached in my pocket - had just enough money for the two drinks – this beautiful girl got up from the table most graciously - said a warm goodbye – within a few minutes was with some one else – did I learn – yes – she was a high-priced call girl – I had no idea I was being set up – I learned the rules real quick - the drinking age in New York state was eighteen – being sixteen and drinking in bars was no big deal – the stage was set for a glorious run of life – I wanted to experience every facet of the word - living – the thrill of winning football games – I so well remember a game we played against Vensenshion High – a moment I will always cherish - the score was 13 to 14 with two minutes to play in our favor – VI got the ball and ran for a touchdown they made the extra point – VI - 20 – Academy 14 – we got the ball back somewhere on our own twenty yard line with less than a minute to play – the next two plays were passes of twenty-some odd yards apiece – with ten seconds left I threw the third pass to my right end Alton Mendelson – touchdown – converted the extra point – VI 20 – Academy 21 – it was that moment always to be remembered – I was blessed with numerous episodes of winning in all sports - basketball – to be able to run like a deer – swimming – baseball – those years playing sandlot ball – ice-skating – roller skating – tennis – horseshoes – badminton – etc. - I wanted to feel – I wanted to touch - life – the inside of me was alone – but the outside of me became full of existence – I saw beyond the moment – but lived in it – I lived at 380 – the house my grandfather built for me was sold – Jack Mayo could not make the payments – I made my own money – in the summer of 1951 – the Korean War was on – could not believe a war was engaged so soon after World War II - I worked for the New York Central Railroad – I worked on a section gang – a section gang consists of about twenty men – we went out each morning to some location where the railroad track was to be fixed – whether we were to move tracks – change ties – tamp – etc. – we worked and worked – I made one dollar and fifty six cents an hour – in the hot summer sun – humidity – and only taking a water break every two hours – here a most interesting frame of my life was to be put in place – out of the twenty of us on the gang plus the boss – I was the only person that was white – it was brought to my attention by my mother who came one afternoon to pick me up – I reflected on what she said – it never occurred to me that I was white – that my coworkers were black – she was crying – saying how sad it was for me to be the only white in the section gang – I told her it was no big deal - we worked under the same hot sun – the same humidity – we exercised our bodies with the same pain - the same duress – day after day – when it rained we all got into the same covered truck – the sweat of our toil permeated the space we occupied - we drank from the same caldron of water – I saw no color – I realized what equality was – I was seventeen – I also became aware that I was to look at every human with equal force – never to put myself ahead or lag behind my fellow being – because of his or her color – or beliefs – I thought about segregation – that feeling of loneliness came into play – I wanted to make a change in our society – but I was much too young – and life was ever so present – so I proceeded to play sports – have my homework done by Linda Carnell – and never stopped the ever so beautiful nightlife – I knew at sixteen once I took a drink I had to get drunk – so I was always careful as to when I was to take a drink – no problem – a sad moment came one fall day in this year of 1951 – my grandmother told me that my mother got into a head on collision some ninety miles away – is almost dead – she was with another man named Harry Query – I knew she was going with a guy – she use to sit in the living room at 380 – smoke her cigarettes - drink her coffee – worry – but this day when my grandmother gave me the news of the accident - much to my regret – I had no feeling – this gave me another moment in my life to feel the dismay - the hurt of not feeling

– I have never forgotten that moment – not good – it seemed such a
short time that elapsed from me when looked out that fourth grade
window in 1944 – saw all those boys in formation in front of the
school – the years passed – the triumphs – the education that the
Academy was trying to give – the many faces to be seen and not
remembered – the ones that will be with me for a lifetime – the teachers that cared - also dared to teach me – the many times I was sent to
the office – reprimanded – the master key I had to all exam rooms –
things I am not so proud of – the cheating that took place in order for
me to pass to each grade – the latitude that was afforded me because
I played sports – the gift - the potential that I had – wasted – I do
remember the class speech I gave the year 1950 in my English class
– it was on racial prejudice – I believed so much in equality for the
human race – yet I could do nothing to propagate it - the lure of life
– the music that played in the clubs – the women – I never drank
because I wanted to get away from life – or to free myself of some
emotional trial – or to drown out my past life – or to run from reality
– or feel sorry for myself – this was my last year of school – I made
Captain in the battalion – I turned nineteen this year – February eighteenth 1952 – I never read a book – never wrote a book report obviously – could not spell – nor could I read too well – here I was in my
last year of high school – a good body – most popular – knew prac-
tically all the other boys and girls in all the high schools – played varsity in all sports – I had the world in my vision – but no idea how to
put the vision into reality – I did not want to go to college – the headmaster of the Academy saw to it that I got a football scholarship to
Springfield College - being the only student in the graduating class
that was not accepted into college – he saw to it I was accepted – he
was also responsible for a full scholarship at the Academy – for playing football - my keen sense of survival carried me through the first
nineteen years of my life – but now I was coming to the real part of
life – the parties were over – the football games were over – along
with basketball – baseball and track – the hundreds of gin mills I
patronized – the dance floors where I fell in love almost every weekend – the smooth sounds of Nat King Cole – Sinatra – Kay Starr -
Tony Bennett - Mr. B. – Joni James – to name a few - looking down

at some facile charmer – to be in love one more time – moment after moment - to be reflected - as the school year was drawing to an end – but not only a school year – nineteen years of life – the struggle – the aloneness – that accompanied each triumph – the sadness that never smiled even when I was laughing – the car accident I got into at two in the morning – how lucky I was to be alive and the people with me – I was driving on a main highway - there was an intersection coming up with a green light for me – as I came across the middle of the intersection – a car came from my left - ran the red – hit me broadside – as Charlie – myself and a girl – lay on the pavement – we saw the light change red for us – every time I go through a green light I am aware of what could happen – above all I remember my grandfather – my godfather – my father – my father at the train station - the tears – so many moments remembered – an eventful excursion my friend Dick Beamish and I had driven from Albany to Miami the summer before - each filled with it's own kind of awareness of life – these moments of life were my teachers – the only formal education I had was at the Albany Academy – school was not for me – I do not remember any of the commencement speech or anything about the graduation – I do remember how quickly the years passed to get where I was at - I worked that summer of 1952 – spent every night with Al and or Charlie – carousing every bar we could envelop – I remember a weekend at Lake George – meeting a girl by the name of Marylyn Lonergan – we danced 'til all hours of the night – she was beautiful – blonde hair – a little bit older than me – my memory is always in the past – so many of these beautiful people - have never grown old in my mind – so many faces from the past come into view – Nancy Trip my first girlfriend – she said I looked like Alan Ladd – in reflecting on these early years of my life – I sometimes wonder if I slowed down a bit what my life would have been like - I knew somehow this was going to be the end of this tenure of my life – I went to Springfield College that fall – when I walked into the dorms – I got that same feeling I had in that orphanage in New York – loneliness – how far I was from that episode of life – but so real at this moment - I make no excuse for any of the actions I partook in – now and for the future - I had every opportunity in my young life that could be afforded me – I was not in sync with me – something was always missing – so going to college was a big mistake – when I first hit the campus at Springfield College – a lonely feeling came over me – the same feeling I had so many times in that orphanage - so many years ago - it was like I was four years old again – I realized that loneliness was going to be a part of my existence - maybe for the rest of my life – I always kept those thoughts to myself – the popularity I experienced thus far in life – the beautiful friends I was blessed with – the most wonderful women I dated – went to dances with – nineteen years of fullness – a spectrum of happenings – from elation to sadness – from being surrounded with friends – to feelings of great loneliness among them - was overwhelming - my desire for sports was gone – my desire to have a higher education was never there – the books I was to get for class – I did not – I could not read them anyway – I cut every class during the week – left Thursday for Albany to be with my friend Al who just lost his girlfriend – needless to say we did a little drinking – we used to talk about old times – we were just teens – me nineteen - Al eighteen – talking about old times – I cannot imagine – like two old fossils – yet there we were in some bar – a thousand years ahead of us – a thousand years behind us – never realizing that each second of our life was going by – well by midsemester I got the report card – one D in English – all the rest were F's – my college days over – I do not think they ever started – I remember seeing the Wizard of Oz – Ray Bolger dancing his way down the yellow brick road – that old soft-shoe – I started a dance career in New York – I wanted to dance in a Broadway show – in the latter part of 1952 the learning process of the soft-shoe was in progress – I worked in Greenwich Village near Fourteenth and Broadway – I worked Saturday and Sunday – made eleven dollars and seventy six cents per weekend – I saved ten dollars for my private soft-shoe lesson – during the week I worked for the United Jewish Appeal for one dollar per hour – all told I made about seventy dollars a week – enough for me to live on – eat and pay rent – my rent was seventy two dollars per month – I was doing real well – I changed jobs around March of 1953 – I became a coat and hat checker – it was run by the Syndicate – mob-affiliated – I worked in all the big hotels – Waldorf Astoria – Carlyle – Lexington – Plaza on Central Park South – Lindys on Broadway – so many stars would come after their shows – I parked cars at the Tavern On The Green – in Central Park – I also checked coats and hats there - about August of 1953 – I got a notice in the mail – it started by saying – "Greetings" – for those of the readers that are not aware of what the phrase –" Greetings" – means – the Army of the United States government wants me – Korea was still going on – my Broadway career was to be put on hold – the nightlife in New York was most beautiful – I remember being able to get a shot of whisky with a beer chaser for twenty-five cents on Sixth Avenue – Broadway bars the best – Fifty Second Street jazz clubs – were my main staple – without being conned by some good looking twenty three or twenty four year old – I now was able to do the conning – I knew most every bar in the Village – life was rich – the experiences of the day I grabbed with a passion – I had a passion for life – I wanted to taste every facet – every corner – light or dark – to feel - to sense - the beat of life – a thirst for knowledge – that was not in books – for I knew I was so delinquent in reading - also in schooling – so every person I came in contact with was my teacher – so here I was the summer of 1953 – I have my draft notice – the Army was not to be – many years prior when I was with my godfather – I used to go to the movies - I saw John Wayne in all those Marine Corps pictures – Sands of Iwo Jima – the Marines on Wake – Midway – Saipan – Corregidor – Okinawa – it was to be for me - to join the Marines – so in the fall of 1953 - at the post office – Albany New York – I was sworn in – Korea had just had a cease fire in August – so they put off my enlistment 'til December or January of 1954 – my choice – so January eleventh came – I boarded a train that morning with a group of recruits – a dissimilar crew – there was a lot of noise – frolicking – as the train moved out of the Albany train station – it seemed we picked up every tough kid that lived on the streets of Albany – there was not a meek one among us – we were on the way to Yemassee – the train station in South Carolina – destination Parris Island – Marine Corps training depot – most notorious – most everyone knew of this place – not because of some romantic refuge – because of the strain – training – of the mind – body – eventually the soul of each – the mystique that surrounded Parris Island – no one person or institution could break the code of silence that pre- vailed on the Island – it was most unique in this respect - our first stop was Poughkeepsie – here we picked another group of recruits – divergent group – yes tough – drinking etc. – on our way to New York – our third group of recruits – than to Jersey – Philadelphia - Baltimore – Washington – by the time we hit North Carolina the train was full of every kind of human being one could imagine – the cacophony – the display of human wreckage – was a sight to behold – people were packing – knives were plentiful – we never slept – but a strange indiscernible phenomenon was about to unfold – about an hour out of Yemassee – a quiet prevailed on the train – no one knew – now - what to expect – the territory was unexplored – the mystique of Parris Island was about to unfold – the train pulled into the station – as it rolled to a stop – we heard voices from the outside – telling us to get off the train in a language known to all plebeians – I knew at that moment I was in for a ride - that was not going to be full of joy – these men that confronted us outside on the platform – were Marines from World War II – they mellowed this onslaught of humanity called - recruits – in about two to three minutes – they pounced on about four or five guys – beat them – stated to the group this is how it works down here in Parris Island – you will do what we want you to do – when we want you to do it – in addition - how to do it – from this moment on - your life belongs to us – the very air you breath belongs to us – you will not eat - sleep – dress – undress – or go to the head little girls - unless we say so – the language we were going to learn was all nautical – head meaning bathroom – floor the deck – wall the bulkhead – etc. – the vocabulary of indecency took on a new meaning – it was not every other word that was profane – it was every word – some I never heard of – it was about two in the morning – we stood on the train platform 'til about 3 a.m. – cold – damp – very dark - waiting for the next move these seasoned Marine veterans were to make – not a sound from any of us that stood there – just waiting – this was just the start – they sure did get our attention – buses came up to the train platform - we were herded into the bus - about fifty or so to each – we traveled a distance - came up on the gates of the Marine Corps depot – Parris Island South Carolina – as I went through the gates the realization of where I was hit me - I remember the feeling so very well – I thought to myself I must do everything in accordance to what the Marine Corps wanted – keep my mouth shut – if enough days pass – I will be taking a bus right through these same gates - as a Marine - private first class – we arrived at a squad bay some time around 3:30 a.m. or so – stood outside 'til about 4 a.m. – at which time we were herded inside the squad bays – stood by the racks – name given for bunks – told we could go to sleep – as we hit the racks - started to go to sleep – the lights went on – shrill sound of a young Marine voice saying – "Hit the deck girls" – this was the beginning of our first day of boot camp – we were herded to the chow hall for breakfast – it wasn't even light out – I do not remember what we had – when it was over we again were herded back to the squad bay – we were given ten minutes to use the head – "head" meaning bathroom – there were over one hundred of us – slight problem – herded back outside - waited - waited – maybe an hour – maybe two – I watched Marine platoons march by – a sight to behold – perfect cadence – showing off a bit as they passed us – coming from a military academy – which I never let anyone know – I knew the manual of arms to perfection – marching – every command – was secondary to me – but under these circumstances no one will ever know or find out anything about the knowledge of my training for six years at the Academy – here we were - civilian clothes – long hair – waiting for the next move of this first day – the smoking lamp was out – which meant we could not smoke – so there we were – no sleep – cold – just waiting – down the path came two Marines – "Sergeant Zimmer is my name - this is PFC Wingate – we are your drill instructors – there are one hundred and seven of you girlie birds" – this saying was not in the vocabulary of indecency – every other word out of his mouth was – he went on to say most of you girls standing here will never make it through boot camp – you will either die or go insane – the ones that do make it will be Marines – part of the greatest fighting organization in the world – did I believe him or not – I did not know – I was not going to ask him for sure – we got our heads shaved – got our issue of clothes – we were Platoon Nineteen – the first night we took cold showers – no toilet paper – the harassment laid on us was something to behold – the first couple of days we lost about five recruits – they just could not take the strain – the pounding on the psyche of each recruit takes its toll – I remember one moment so vividly to this day – we were outside the chow hall – I looked at my watch – it was a quarter to twelve – I watched the second hand going around – they can do anything they want to me anytime – but the one thing they cannot do - is stop time from going by – if enough seconds pass – this period will be over – but for now - little sleep – running everywhere – ten minutes to eat – learning how to march – self defense – how to kill – learning all there is to know about my M1 rifle – the demoralizing – the debilitating atmosphere that surround all of us – took three recruits one day – section eight – meaning one goes crazy – those poor boys as I remember – I felt so sad for each – a strange look on each of the faces – they were just out of reality – Sergeant Zimmer told us this is what is going to happen to each of us - as time goes by – the training most arduous – after about three weeks Platoon Nineteen was marching fairly well – doing the manual of arms – able to take our M1's apart and put them back together with ease – by this time we lost about fifteen of our recruits – I saw them go home shaved heads with each – brown pants - purple shirt – so sad – I saw new recruits come in – so glad I was not there – as the weeks moved on Platoon Nineteen became more proficient – Sergeant Zimmer never cut us any slack – my serial number 1465048 sir – I still remember so well – as the days went into weeks – so did the weeks move into months – little sleep – twenty to twenty-two hour days – we were now marching as a platoon – new recruits looked at us with envy – Sergeant Zimmer these last couple of weeks began to instill in us the spirit of the Marine Corps – this is the indefinable fiber a Marine has – no other way to explain it – a bearing that each of us will carry for the rest of our lives – here we were seventy recruits left out of one hundred and seven – we weathered all that Parris Island had to expose – and then some – the last day we were in our clean pressed uniform – we marched to the chow hall for the last time – Sergeant Zimmer a most proud Marine – he did his job well – we were well-trained – combat ready – as we passed other recruits on the way to the chow hall – we could here other drill instructors say to their recruits –"When you become Marines this is how you will look" that feeling of pride came over us – the accomplishment – the overwhelming sense of joy – the memories of the tired - tormented – harassed – ridiculed – abused - bodies – were but a blur – I passed my twenty-first birthday while in boot camp – I weighed one hundred and seventy nine pounds – not one ounce of fat – I could lift a hundred pound sea bag on my shoulder with one arm – I was in perfect condition - that first morning standing in the damp cold of Parris Island – to this day three months later – is with me for my lifetime – Sergeant Zimmer marched us to a drop-off section - where we were to be picked-up - bused to the train station Yemassee – he stood on a platform - faced us squarely – he spoke " You came here as boys - now you are Marines - God be with you" there was a quiet – he got down from the platform – started walking down the street out of sight – there is a feeling inside of me that has never left – I went through those gates – those same gates I passed three months prior – reflected those same thoughts as when I arrived on the Island – it came to pass – I had a two week leave in which I went to New York to visit my mother – I remember how proud she was of me – while I was there visiting - for some unknown reason I wanted to go back to that orphanage I was in many years prior – so my mother – myself - took off for Yonkers - which was only a short distance away from the Bronx where my mother lived – we came to the bottom of this hill which I remembered so well – around sixteen or seventeen years have passed since I ran down that hill crying profusely for my Aunt Babe to take me with her – the same amount of time also - that I took that long walk up that hill with the snow - wind – tears – in my face to the rec hall – here I was twenty-one years old – a lifetime had passed – my godfather – my grandfather died – more schools – more flunked grades – could not read – shifted from one place to another – even made one more orphanage in Troy New York – learned how to be self-sufficient – sports – now a Marine - gifted – I was gifted in so many ways – yet as we drove up that hill – I was that small boy again – it all came back to me – I never let my mother know what I was feeling – she was most quiet also as we drove to the rec hall – we got out of the car – I was dressed in my uniform - of dress greens – as it was called – we went inside - there I was so many years ago – these young kids playing – much sadness filled my soul – they looked at me with wonderment – my instincts felt the aloneness of each boy – we asked for the person in charge – my eyes met the eyes of Sister Kerbin – only this time I was not that little boy she could pick up by the nape of the neck because I snickered at the quick movements of an older boy getting whipped – I stood a foot taller than she – she was old - wrinkled – she didn't quite remember me – I asked for that women Mary – the one that would strap us - if one sound was uttered - going to bed at night – Sister Kerbin said she no longer worked here – I asked her if I could go up to the dormitory for a moment – she said yes - I went through a hallway that led upstairs – there I saw the corner where I spent hours weeping – up the stairs I went - as if not a day had been missed these past years – into the dorm where all the beds were made – I stood for a moment in the still of the silence – the smell was the same – it was empty - yet I could hear the murmur – ever so softly – of the souls that passed through – like me – ever so lonely – yesterday was to-day – but to-day was so many years ago – we left that orphanage – the memory remains – I never went back – nor did I ever hold it as a crutch to manipulate any thing or any one to favor me – nor did I ever blame my mother or grandmother – I was what I am – I never felt sorry for myself – nor carry any burden of my past – the only thing I carried with me was loneliness – at twenty-one years old – I never made an attempt to allow my past to run my present - Korea did not resume – I was off to a base in Jacksonville Florida – here I would spend three months preparing to be assigned to a Marine air wing – the nightlife would begin – the bars in Jacksonville were plentiful – I pulled liberty every chance I could get – liberty meaning a pass off the base – I made eighty-two dollars a month – in the bars I could con my way to beautiful nights – on base I forged liberty cards – sold them for five dollars - loaned money - three dollars for five - at payday – I had a lot of little business on the side – one of my dear friends whose name was Singleton – from New York – he was black – I never realized that he was black – never gave it any credence – he was my

44

friend - we walked into this bar one day on a Saturday afternoon – went up to the bar and ordered two beers – the bartender said he would serve me – "…but not that nigger" – I could not believe what I heard – stunned – I told the bartender to serve my friend – he would not serve him – I told the bartender if he did not serve my friend – I'll tear this bar apart – using much of the vocabulary of indecency – we were twenty-one - just out of Parris Island – ready to kill – a fight meant nothing to us – this scene felt a little different in some way – about six men that were sitting down at the other end of the bar stood up – at which time the bartender said once again – he would serve me but not Singleton – at that time I looked at Singleton – looked at the six guys – "We can take them" – I said – Singleton looked at me said – "Maybe – but let's get out of here" – I never realized at the time I was in the South – the North and South do things a little differently when it comes to color – I remembered at that moment when I worked on the section gang for the railroad – my mother crying as I got into the car – saying I was the only white boy out of eighteen or twenty men – I remembering saying there was no difference between any of us – I also remember the speech on racial prejudice I gave in my English class four years prior - this was the real poison – this was a real moment – this was not a game – reality – I never heard about Martin Luther King Jr. – the only people I knew of were Jackie Robinson – I knew of Jesse Owens - Joe Louis was my idol all through the forties I loved him – I stood up for equality that day - in that bar - in Jacksonville Florida – I was willing to put my life on the line for what I believed in – the ideology was tucked away in my being – the process of learning a philosophy - a way of life - was not on my agenda – the world was big - I had a lot of living to do – I met a girl in New York after boot camp about three weeks before this episode – her name was Bobbie De Maria – she was a designer of children's clothes – I never thought much of having a relationship at the time when I was in New York – but I started to think of her while training here in Jacksonville – I remember how well we received each other – how she cared about me – not one discomforting thought – here I was twenty-one years old she cared about me – in a way that was most unselfish – she was beautiful – slender – dark hair – about five foot six inches tall – willowy – with dark piercing eyes – we would dance 'til the bars closed - she was most understanding – That Old Black Magic was and still is a song – is most apropos to the way our feelings ran – pure – most clear – there were many times I went on liberty in Jacksonville – the bars were many – the drinking was most prevalent - I heard of a Naval base in New Jersey called Lakehurst – lighter-than-air dirigible – a very famous base known for a horrible tragedy back in the thirties – a dirigible named the Hindenburg blew up killing many – if I passed with high grades here in Jacksonville Airmen Preparatory School – I could have my choice of my second school to go to – New York was seventy miles from Lakehurst – it was a parachute rigger school – learning how to pack chutes – survival equipment – etc.- for the Marine air wing – air-to-ground support – so I got myself a high grade and off to Lakehurst I went – there was much pride in wearing the Marine uniform – Korea did not break out – the war seemed in check – when I arrived in Lakehurst I could not wait to get liberty – for the next several months I went to school during the day – liberty at night in New York with Bobbie De Maria – the clubs - the bars - the dancing 'til all hours of the night – I would get back to the base around four a.m. – start all over again the next day – I thought this time period of my life would last forever – I was not cognizant of time passing – only living in the moment – thirsting for each day's experience life had to offer – the loneliness inside of me always prevailed – this I was aware of – but by no means allowed it to infiltrate in me or dominate my being – nor did I shut the feelings down that existed – nor did I make any effort to escape – through alcohol – drugs – the nightlife – the clubs - etc. – the loneliness that I carried with me was a part of my make-up – I never spoke to anyone about these feelings – here I was twenty one years old – an accomplished athlete – Marine – career to go back to in New York – a beautiful girl that I was going with – a lust for life – a keen sense of survival – I could talk with kings – I could mingle with plebeians – yes the little boy of five in that orphanage was still prevalent – with the snow on my face – the tears in my eyes – that long walk up that hill to the rec hall – I never hid from the responsibility of self – well the months passed – the time came for me to be shipped to another Marine base in Florida - for the past nine months I saw only one girl – the feelings inside me were feelings I had never felt prior – I was a very lucky young man to have someone care for me - someone to have such pronounced feelings - to be with me – the same feelings ran through me – being inexperienced in this pocket of life – I did not know what to do – I had two years plus facing me in the Marines – I did not know where that was going to take me – the lure of life – the lights of the night – the fast lane – the intrigue of the unknown – the clubs – the gin mills – I have yet to visit – here on one hand I have an entity that may pass but once in a lifetime – Miami was too much waiting for me – so off I went – not without having that lonely feeling creep back into my being – I kept thinking about Bobbie De Maria – I pushed the feelings aside – Miami South Beach was in full swing December 1954 – the nightlife was something to behold – my friend Charlie Stone from my school days was here with me – we patronized a club by the name of Rocking M B Lounge on Collins Avenue – a guy by the name of TNT played the drums – backed up by two horns and a bass – they had the stage in the center of the bar – I can still hear the sounds of Night Train – all those magnificent jazz tunes I used to hear on Fifty Second Street New York – we drank 'til four – went to afterhours clubs drank 'til six a.m. – went back to the base - mustered at seven – did as little work as my hangover would allow – at these times I knew a little bit of the dog that bit me would help my condition – for by this time of my life I was well-schooled in alcohol – I was coming up on twenty- two years old – I have no idea how many times I was drunk – how many bars I drank in – how many times I was sick – how many nights I did not come home – how many parties I passed out at – how many times I had the DTs – how many blackouts I had - the realization of alcohol depriving me of any kind of athletic career whatsoever or any schooling for that matter was not present – I was young - strong - virile – my drinking career started with a little wine – a little sherry in my eggnog – I drank every kind of liquor that was made – every kind of beer – cheap – expensive – I was a connoisseur – what to drink – how to drink – where to drink – dealing with the day after – or the day that never was – I was most secure when it came to alcohol – I believe at this time of my life I was an accomplished virtuoso in every facet there was to be offered about alcohol – my dear friend Charlie and I had some beautiful times together – we must have hit every club on Collins Avenue at one time or another before he left because of illness – he was gone but the nightlife was ever so present – I was a cabana boy on weekends – I also took care of some runaway delinquent boys around ages fourteen through sixteen – being in the Marine Corps it was an easy task - they listened or my wrath – I would teach them things of life – how to survive – how to be aware of one's surroundings – but most of all discipline – I would not tolerate misbehavior – I would treat them like young boots coming to Parris Island – they responded – one day I took them - five or six to Miami Beach - South Shore – there was a two-or-so mile jetty going out into the ocean – it was a beautiful day as we started on the two-mile jagged rock journey out into the ocean – it took about an hour and one-half to get three-quarters of the way out – at which time I began to notice the surf was getting a bit choppy – I terminated our ploy to reach the end of the jetty – they were disappointed – but obeyed – we started back very cautiously – I was there to help each boy over the rocks – twenty minutes later the surf was really coming in – I now kept the boys real close – we had one treacherous low spot we had to pass – there was no protection from the waves coming in – I knew we had to overcome this pass in order to get to shore – when we got to this juncture I guided and lifted each boy to safety – when I turned around to get the last boy – whose name I still remember – Chuck Bennet – he was in the water being bashed up against these rocks – he did not wait for me – the other boys were yelling – telling me what was happening – they were panicking – in the most direct order I ever gave or ever will give – I told the boys to stay put – I turned to see Chuck – he was immobile – his body was being thrashed against the rocks – like a rag doll – I had a second or two to decide what course to take – if I did not get him now he would be lost - another wave hit – at that instance with one arm I grabbed his arm – in one motion I lifted his body into mine – tucked him inside of my chest cavity – braced myself for the next wave – it came – Chuck was still in my chest cavity – I lifted him up to safety – he was a bloody mess – I also was a bloody mess – cut by the coral rock - Chuck was in shock – could not talk or move – I carried him - at the same time guided the other four boys to the shore – Chuck recovered – I got coral poisoning – was laid up for awhile – I pulled many people out of the ocean – at this period of my life – I guess I was lucky too - one weekend I saw this woman in a leopard-skin one-piece bathing suit – I introduced myself – she to me – her name Louise Lobdell – she was a beautiful women – as we talked I realized how uneducated I was – how educated she was – a few days passed – we kept talking – with all the education she had - she was a beach comber – she loved life – a free spirit – in 1955 it was unheard of – nonetheless here we were – I was so impressed with her knowledge – her vocabulary was something to behold – so I asked her to teach me – I told her I couldn't read so I had to learn verbally – Louise was thirty-six – we started – most of the words in my vocabulary to-day are from this time period – she taught me about painters – took me to museums – took me to Havana Cuba before Castro – we too shared the clubs – Fontainebleau in Miami – Tropicana in Cuba – great names to be remembered – books – scientists – world-famous places – oceans – lakes – mountains – every day something new – how to order food in a fine restaurants - I was a good student – I knew I was to learn these entities if I were to accomplish anything in life – the time came when she had to leave for New York City – she presented me with a Webster's Dictionary – I used to make up words when I first met her - she would ask me what they meant – I would make up some definition for the fictitious word – I would say – "When I use a word – I mean it to mean what I mean it to mean – neither more nor less" – she scribed that phrase in the front of the dictionary she gave me – Humpty Dumpty said it to Alice – in Alice In Wonderland - the book – she left – we wrote – many times – in the next few months – five or six letters a week – 1956 was coming around – I was in a club in one of the hotels on Collins Avenue South Beach – in the club they had an ice show – I was having a few drinks as the show began – I had a front row seat – every time one of the skaters went by she would give me a look – the show ended – backstage I went – introduction by name – Janet Collins was her name – a beautiful woman – about five-foot eight – dark long hair – piercing deep set eyes – there was a band in the club – I asked her to dance – we were on that dance floor – I looked into those eyes – I had that old feeling – I couldn't believe what was running through me – could it happen twice in a lifetime – to have these moments – to feel - to sense with such clarity – to want to be with someone and someone only – a lifetime was beginning - yet unknown to me - ending – for I got orders to ship out – destination Iwakuni Japan – I will be gone a year – the month before I left Janet and I were inseparable – danced - cried – I will never forget the song we danced to that last night – the song - When Your Lover Has Gone – that lonely feeling inside of me - ever so deep - was most present – to California for a month – left San Diego headed for Japan – there were five thousand Marines on this troop ship – the racks were stacked six high – when morning chow was over – after waiting two hours in line – I got back in line for noonday chow – thus was the day's agenda – cleaned our rifles again and again – there was one obstacle that had to be overcome by me – many years ago when I was sent to the Sutton farm around seven years old – one of my chores was to empty the night's human waste into the outhouse – the picture of the pile of human waste in the outhouse never left me – I went up to use the head aboard ship - about a day or two into the twenty-one day crossing of the Pacific – I could not believe what I saw – toilets without any seats – maybe three hundred with rails separating each – that was bad – but what made it really unbearable was ninety percent of the toilets were full of waste – the stigma from my chores on the farm has never left – we reached Japan - on to the new base – it would take two weeks for mail to get to the States conversely two weeks from the States to Japan – I was getting letters every day from Janet and writing letters each day – they were beautiful letters – it seemed my feelings were as strong in Japan as they were Stateside – I would go on liberty – drink much – but no dates – about two months passed by – I received a letter from Janet with a different dimension – needless to say it sure did shake me up – I got an emergency leave – wound up in Wildwood New Jersey where she was doing a show – confronted her – yes she met a trumpeter in Detroit – devastated I was – I had to fly back to Japan after a couple days – a stop over in

Treasure Island - San Francisco – my very being was broken – every night I would pull a liberty – there was a street in downtown San Francisco I would hang out at - not a good area – a lot of bars - far from fancy – I would be drunk every night – back to the Treasure Island in the morning – only to start all over again – one morning I got back to the base – the sergeant of arms told me I had to report to sickbay – so off to sickbay I went – much to my chagrin and my dismay – the doctor in charge told me I had a problem with drinking – I could not believe what I heard – so the doctor shipped me to a Navy hospital in Oakland – as I was walking toward the ward I was assigned to – I stopped outside – looked up – the sign read – Psycho Ward Eight – I could not believe what I saw – twenty-two years old – here I was being committed to a psycho ward for drinking – I had all my faculties about me – I could stop drinking any time I wanted – as I walked through the doors into the ward – there before me were people around thirty-five years old – Navy chiefs – some Marines – a few young people – one I knew from Miami – I asked him how do I get out of here – he said I would have to stay a minimum of thirty days – in three days I would meet the head psychiatrist – that I would have to go to these Alcoholics Anonymous meetings each day – when I was in high school it was advised that I go to Alcoholics Anonymous – I never went – what a predicament I was in – three days passed - in I went to see the head psychiatrist – this I will never forget – I asked if I could be permitted to speak first – he said "Go right ahead Raymond" – "Sir I do not belong here" – these were the words out of my mouth – the look on his face was all- knowing – saying very simply – "Yes I know" – I realized at that moment I made a mistake – I could not take it back – so here I was locked in for a time – everything in the ward was suicide-safe – push-button showers – toilets – wash basins – meds – which I did not take – these people in this ward had problems with drinking – I went to my first Alcoholics Anonymous meeting on the ward – we would sit around in a circle - talk about experiences that happened to us – I just wanted to get out of this place – I could forge liberty cards – so each night I would hit the bars – during the day go to the meetings – I could identify with almost all the stories – I had the blackouts - DTs – etc. – I even had those crazy episodes – like meeting a good-looking girl in one of those dive gin mills – remembering only leaving the bar going into a blackout – waking up in the morning - only to find a man beside me – introducing himself as Manual – I did not tell this story for a long time – nothing went on between us – that is the story – I spent twenty-eight days in the ward - all those meetings – finally got out – back to Treasure Island – a few more bars in San Francisco – then off to Japan – back to Iwakuni – had about ten more months to go before I got discharged – it was 1956 – I was a buck sergeant – making one hundred and forty dollars a month – liberty every night – when four o'clock rolled around I was off to the clubs on the Strip – I walked into this one club – had a few drinks – I asked this one girl to dance – we danced – 'til the place closed – her American name was Nina – she spoke very little English – what little Japanese I knew – we got along fine – these girls that worked in the clubs – were prostitutes – Nina was no different – once a month she would be with the colonel of the base – as time went by she would always feel so bad when I could not be with her on that particular night – there was something about her that was so beautiful – she was brought up in Kobe Japan – which is somewhere near Hiroshima – she would describe to me how the atomic bomb went off – the beautiful colors – the mushroom – then she would put her face in her hands with the deepest of sorrow – realizing it was a bomb – the horror of what was – her whole demeanor changed – as she wept softly – the feelings that ran through her soul – the helplessness she displayed – the wound of the experience that would never mend – I sat - listened to her aura – I could understand everything that was inside her – very few words were spoken – a tie – a link – a connection – a bond - that was sealed for a lifetime – I held her with the care of the loneliness that embodied my being – the next few months we were filled with trips to different places in Japan – ground zero in Hiroshima – the city was nothing in 1956 – ground zero was nothing but weeds – nothing left of the city – remembering the United States was occupying Japan at the time – not too much building was going on – Nina and I would spend much time together – the nightlife we shared – the weekends – I did not realize feelings were so close for each other – we would share everything – she would cook – we would go out to movies together – foreign movies with Japanese subtitles – I did not understand a word – I made a trip to Hong Kong – China – at the time Ray Milland won best actor at the Academy Awards for his portrayal of an alcoholic in The Lost Weekend – when I hit Hong Kong – the bars were new – the music was unbelievable – the nights were long – the days were short – I had a lost week – woke up in some storefront surrounded by a group of Chinese ready to pounce on me – I did escape with much quickness – went back to my hotel with two bottles of whisky one in each hand – at which time I barged in this girl's room by the name of Helen - like John Wayne – sat down at a mirrored make-up table with my hands grasping each bottle of whisky – I put my head down between my arms still holding the whisky bottles – the next morning I woke up still holding the two whisky bottles – alone – wondering what happened – Hong Kong – was the only city one could visit in China – the rest of the country was called Red China – off-limits – I did manage to buy beautiful bolts of silk for Nina back in Japan to make clothes for herself – I remember the airport bar in Formosa – nine hours in that bar – watching Chiang Kai-shek planes take off – there was Okinawa – Midway – Wake – before I hit Japan – finally got back to Iwakuni – seems to me I lost a little time in these bars along life's path – I do also recollect a lost three days in Honolulu – when it was a territory – I was back with Nina – she sure did love the silks – we used to plan for my last day in Japan – how she would come to the base in full dress kimono – that was a long way off – the months did seem to go fast – the summer into the fall of 1956 – when November rolled around I realized I had about thirty days left in Japan - I got some lonely feelings that surfaced through my being – Nina was a big part of my life by this time – we verbally told each other we loved one another – we had experienced almost a year of life together – it was a joy to see her – be with her – her actions spoke so loud – she was always calm – radiantly beautiful – soft-spoken – most direct – no deceitfulness in her being – there was not a trace of selfishness in any moment we shared together – her eyes told the story of how she felt toward me – I was aware enough that I felt the very core of her soul – I was twenty-three years old on the brink of

something most profound – most intense – my only thought was of
her – her only thought was of me – singleness of thought for each –
I tried to stop time – but that second hand on my watch kept moving
– the same second hand that moved that day in Parris Island three
years prior – I pondered taking her back to the States – to no avail –
should I stay here with her – I had to go back to the States – get discharged – then back to Japan – a dilemma to say the least – I do not
think either one of us saw this coming – we were living the life -
never realizing there was an end – the feelings were overpowering –
inside of me that little boy of four - crying - with that lonely feeling
- once again - was most prevalent – well the time came – that last day
– December 1956 – this was the day Nina was to come to the base in
full dress kimono – we were to have one last party – compliments of
my Marine Corps buddies – I went down to the gates where I was to
meet her – as I approached the gates - I saw her – radiantly beautiful
– in full dress kimono – I took her hand – we walked to the hall where
the party was – everyone cheered as we walked in – a strange quiet
resided inside of me – I did not drink this day – nor did Nina – she
said so very little - as did I – the festiveness of the party had no effect
on either of us – the emotions of the past year ran through each of us
– I got permission to take her home – we said our goodbyes – we got
into a cab – on the way to her apartment she told the cab to stop –
said to him "Jota mati" – which means wait – she came out of a small
store – her words to me were – "Presento" – she handed me a small
box which I opened – in it was a cigarette lighter – her words to me
were – To you - so you never forget me" – the tears came as we drove
on to her apartment – not one word was spoken – we went into her
room she sat on the edge of her bed – I sat in a chair in front of her –
not one word was spoken – yet volumes spilled into our hearts – permeated the space we occupied – I stood up went to the bamboo sliding door - stopped – I could not get myself to open it – so there I
stood – I turned around - looked at her – her eyes looking toward the
floor – her face so beautiful – the tears now so quietly running down
her face – she looked at me and uttered these words – "I never see
you again" – I answered – "No" – she then said "Sayonara" – I
looked at her for the last time – I said "Sayonara" – I slid the door

open - closed it ever so gently behind me – my heart - my very being was to be harnessed - with this overpowering view of two people - with a love to last a lifetime – yet never to see one another again – the empty feelings that swept through my conscious and unconscious mind – the loneliness I was most acclimated to - ran deep – there will be no escaping this episode of my life – as the ship left Yamaha Bay – the distance grew – as the island of Japan faded – nothing left but water between me – and the lasting memory - that will become a beacon of purity - that could have been – I reached San Francisco eleven days later – it was the end of December 1956 – I was to be discharged from a Navy base in Brooklyn - called Floyd Bennet Field – it was four in the morning when I reached the base – I had my sea bag with all my gear - etc. – as I went through the gates – I started my last walk to a barracks – it was dark - cold - the fog was in - so I could not see ten feet in front of me – I reflected back to when I walked up that hill in the blinding snow in the orphanage – with the tears running down my face – I saw my grandfather pick me up – I saw my godfather wipe the blood from my forehead – I saw my father leave me at the train station – never to see me again – I saw the little kids at the orphanage come up to me in wonderment - when I went back to visit them in my Marine uniform – I saw Nina with the tears in her eyes – I still hear her words – "I never see you again" – over and over – it was a lonely walk up to the barracks that morning – I was finishing my tour of duty – three years of my life – looking back I realized how quickly the time had passed - a new life would start – I got an honorable discharge January 10th 1957 – I served 1096 days - came out a buck sergeant - I no longer wanted to do the old soft shoe – instead I turned my interest to an acting career – under the GI bill I enrolled in the American Academy of Dramatic Arts – to support myself I got a hack license – I drove a cab in New York for the next few years – New York had changed somewhat – the Fifty-Second Street jazz clubs were a thing of the past – Sixth Avenue was about to change its face – a shot of whisky and a beer for twenty-five cents was a thing of the past – the bars on Eighth Avenue were still in session – as were the bars in Greenwich Village – I had just about everything going for me – there were many cab stories to be told – many happenings that happened – my story is not about me and my escapades – it is about feelings that run through the soul – with all that was going on - the prevalent feeling of loneliness prevailed – there was no escape – nor did I want to escape from such feelings – as the first six months were passing – which was equivalent to the first year of schooling – I was invited back to my second six months – we did many plays – I learned my craft well – 1958 was about to roll in – things seemed in good order – I was working as a cab driver – I was twenty-five years old come February eighteenth – I had met a girl at the Academy – we got married this year of 1958 – a little bit about the beginning of this marriage – remembering the first time she and I drove up to her parent's home in Connecticut – as we turned into this quarter-mile driveway - flanked by two ponds - up to this most beautiful home behind a circular drive – fronted by two magnificent oak trees – it was an eighty-five acre estate – a most beautiful piece of property – there would never be a worry of any sort for the rest of my life – did I have good motives or oblique motives – I remember our wedding day in the church when the priest presiding asked – "Is there any one present who thinks these two people should not be together in holy matrimony" – at that moment I knew I should have stood up – I should have stood up but I did not – we were married – the reception under a huge pink tent on that eighty-five acre estate – the money – the property – the sixty-foot yacht – the new car – the dinners in the finest restaurants in New York – Connecticut – the credit cards – homes that would be paid for – a job in any field I wanted would be subsidized – in fact anything I desired would be available – there was one small catch – I had to be a good husband – at the time it did not seem like such a bad trade-off - so I proceeded - I drove my cab weeknights – followed my career during the days – we lived in the Bronx – went to Connecticut weekends – I would leave Sunday afternoons to work at night in New York – one Sunday morning I looked out a bedroom window from the two- story house – what I saw was most disconcerting to me – all of the family were cleaning – sweeping – polishing – etc. etc. – were they doing this out of obligation – the father-in-law paid for everything – as I looked out - I realized I could not be part of the atmosphere that prevailed – so off I would go each Sunday to drive my cab in New York – the thoughts were many – I could not buy into the process of being a "yes boy" – in a very short time I realized I could not be bought – every dream I had of my future came to a quick dead-end – I knew in my heart that a mistake was made - that moment in that chapel when I should have stood up – came to pass more than once – could I rectify a mistake – time would tell – I did shows in and around New York – but the atmosphere that surrounded my personal life had to change – 1959 my wife became pregnant – at that time I was making plans to go to California for television was becoming most prevalent – the summer of 1959 while she was pregnant we took off for Hollywood – things looked promising – that fall she went back to New York to get ready for the birth – I would follow the latter part of October – I also knew that I was going to move to California soon after the baby was born – November was here – I stood in front of a baby boy in the hospital at 1 a.m. – incredulous – were my feelings – wonderment – his name was Raymond – I reflected on my life as I looked through the glass into the nursery – he was going to be able to read – have a stable life – never feel loneliness - these were my only thoughts – was I going to be able fulfill the destiny of this boy – I knew my drinking was becoming more obsessive – my desire to leave New York - go to California – the discord between my wife and myself was budding – there were many factors that curbed the ideals that were good – as I looked at this young soul – there was a sorrow in my being – reality - I never ran away from the aspect of truth – I knew the score – I was behind – I also took chances – so in the summer of 1960 off to California we went – got a small house in the Silver Lake area – I began to work a short time after I arrived – by 1961 I was working as an actor – supplementing my career with a multitude of jobs – for by this time child number two was born – the drinking progressed every day – every night I would go to bars 'til 2 a.m.– one night I came home to get money to continue my night – as I got to my car my wife was yelling – "who is that person in the car with you" – I shouted back in the middle of the night – "no one is in the car – what is the matter with you" – I got into the car and as I was driving off - the girl sitting next to me said – "who was that" – I said with out a beat –

"who was what – I did not hear anything" - my demeanor was changing – my talent was still good – at times other thoughts would come in my head while delivering lines in a television show – this was not good - I did many shows – 1962 – 1963 – 1964 – the bills were backing up – a girl was born 1963 – I do not remember what hospital she was born in – nor another boy in 1964 – by 1965 my talent level was diminishing – at this time we were living in a beautiful home in Tarzana south of the Boulevard – as is said – but the dark side of life was following me – I had been stopped for drunk driving so many times it got to be boring – I could not retain lines any more – I was not a good father – I would wake my two older boys up in the middle of the night asking where their little bank was – to take their money so I could buy a bottle of gin – being a husband was nowhere to be found – being a provider was in the same category – the lies that were needed to perpetuate my existence – the self-delusion that was creeping into my being – the principles I stood for as a young boy were being supplanted – fears – paranoia – deceit – dishonesty was my mode of operation – there was so much going on in my head – I could no longer change my direction even if I chose to – I believed fully that I was on a track going nowhere – I could not tell anyone – my wife and I would try to iron out the many differences we had - to no avail – I was thirty-three years old February 1966 – the first part of the year I got a job on a show at 20th Century Fox – I remember going up to the guard at the gate – telling him my name – asking him what show I was on – he told me it was Peyton Place - I went to the sound stage – I went to the second assistant and told him I never received a script – he got one for me – I started to learn my lines – when it came time for the first scene to be shot – I could not remember one line – they had to get cue cards for me – in New York ten years prior – I could learn four hundred fifty lines in three days – perform in four – here I stood – firstly - could not remember what show I was on – secondly - could not remember one line of dialogue – alcohol was part of my life – not good – the hundreds of times I got drunk – the hundreds of bars – the blackouts – the DTs – the memory loss – the fun I had - that was going to last a lifetime – the drunk-driving stops over thirty-five – maybe more – the tail end of 1966 – I got a job on the stage – it was a big musical in a big house - capacity over three thousand – What Makes Sammy Run was the name of the play – maybe this was my last chance to redeem my career – I worked most arduously on the part – in my heart I knew I was not the actor I was in New York or even when I first came to Hollywood – we rehearsed for three weeks – the show was to run two weeks – we opened – the show was a success – I knew I did not have the pure talent level I once had – the ensemble came out each night to watch Frank Gorshin and myself work – everyone thought we were so great – everyone except me – please understand Frank was great – I was the one who knew another level could be had by me – it was a Saturday night – over three thousand people in the audience – including the author of the play – Budd Shulberg – this was theatre-in-the-round – on this Saturday night I stood in the back of the theatre waiting for my cue to go on – the energy in the theatre was electrifying – I had been - in years past – encompassed with moments like this – that I was witnessing – I said a prayer for the first time in many years – it went like this – "Please God let me have my talent back – let me feel the awareness of the situation – let me feel the purity - the clarity I once had as a young actor – I promise from this moment on – I will not drink anymore – I will be a good faithful husband – I will be a good father – a provider for the children" – I think I would have sold my soul to the devil for this one moment – so here I was standing in the wings – my cue came – down the aisle I went – I hit the stage – the moment was here – the scene took off as it was meant to be – fulfilled to capacity – I made my exit – as I was walking back through the aisle from where I came – the audience began to clap - it lasted for several minutes – I exited the theatre to my dressing room – the applause still in my ears – at that moment I knew my talent had returned – a joyful feeling encompassed me – my prayer was answered to the fullest – the bargain I made with God was a reality – my turn was next – that night after the show I started drinking gin – drank 'til all hours of the morning – forgot all about the deal I made with God – so here I was six in the morning - most intoxicated – I sleep for a few hours – I had a matinee – so off I went to the theater – my cue came again – on stage I came – only this time – the shell – of what was left – the collapse of my being – I knew I was at the tail-end of my career – even though I was only thirty-three years old – the talent that I once possessed was no longer – I could not retain lines – the purity of an accomplished actor can only be achieved by the total focus on the situation at hand – no interference whatsoever – this I knew – this I also knew I did not have – I am thirty-three years old – the obsession to drink was just that – singleness of thought – there was no place for me to go but down – I made beautiful furniture years prior – yet I could not cut a board - forty–five inches long – I remember that so well – alcohol now was going to take a part of me – not a little at a time - but in leaps – the obsession to drink overpowered me – I would give in – start to drink – off I would go to some bar – some sordid place – Skid Row many times – I had drank on many Skid Rows in many cities across the country - world too – San Francisco – Chicago – Miami – New York – Philadelphia – Tokyo – Hong Kong – Albany New York - I never left the airport in Formosa – woke up in a lot of strange places – I've had guns drawn on me – broken beer bottles staring at me – the alleys I woke up in – subways I passed out in 'til dawn – by this time of my life I had drank just about all forms of alcohol made – my main substance was gin – straight gin – it seemed to get me downtown fast – once I took a drink – it was over – I had to satiate the craving – the stage was set – only not in a theatre – in life - I did not know what the future held for me – 1967 came - here I was thirty-four years old – unable to work – my talent long gone – a prevalent obsession to drink – I went to supermarkets to steal bottles of alcohol many many times – the intake of alcohol began to decrease – what once took a bottle of gin or whisky to put me under – took only a few ounces – blackouts were most rampant – auditory DTs - I wandered the streets many a night – I would wake up one of my children – forcing him to give me his money he saved – because I needed a drink – paranoia set in – I thought everyone was after me – there was no escaping the reality of the nothingness that surrounded me – the life at home was non-existent – the obsession to drink was all-consuming – debts were mounting – the milk bill – I remember - was over a hundred and fifty dollars – my physical being was disintegrating as the months came and went – I was beginning to bleed internally – I remember having worms – sores on my body that would not heal – I poured gin over them thinking the alcohol would heal them – I would write myself letters – when the mailman came I would be devastated from the news that was coming in the letter – I would get all emotional over the news that was to be – I cannot remember what was in the letter as far as what I wrote – no recollection whatsoever - I would receive the letter - turn start to walk back to the house – at which time a voice inside me would say – "Ray - why are you getting so upset over this letter - you wrote it to yourself" – I could not digest that thought – incredulous – my mind seemed to flip into reality – flip out of reality – I would make phone calls to Universal Studios – to Ann Baxter – I knew she was blackballing me – keeping me from working at the studios – I would dial six or seven digits and hang up – I would realize they were arbitrary numbers going nowhere – again that voice – "Ray – you don't know Ann Baxter" – again unbelieving – how could my mind drift so far from reality – the calls - the letters - would continue – the same pattern – the same voice – my mind would reflect moments gone - the bars – sewers really – to capture a moment of the past – to have a feeling of peace – the misconducts – the lies – the cons - the infidelities – the impurities of my soul – the dishonesty that surrounded my heart – the selfishness that consumed my very being – loneliness – loneliness beyond – I am that little boy in the orphanage - walking up that hill in the blinding snow storm with the tears running down my face – how beautiful - how simple - it was twenty years prior – to the complexities of now – I am still that little boy with the tears on my face – will the loneliness ever leave – the pictures of my grandfather – my godfather – of my father – I needed their wisdom so badly - the hope I had as a young boy – the desire to succeed – the gifts I had – the gifts I lost – some of the thoughts that have nourished my soul - the anguish - that is prevailing in my spirit - I am coming to my end – there is no way I can undo what has passed – it was 1968 I believe – my wife became pregnant – I believe it was somewhere in the eighth month of her pregnancy – I cannot even remember the last two children that were born – where or when - we were in the upstairs bedroom – an argument was ensuing – she looked at me with such distain – "I hate you - I hate you" – she said over and over – with each "hate" she pounded her stomach – "I hate you - and I have to have your child" - at that moment I told her – "You are tampering with something you should not tamper with" – made no difference – what have I done to make her suffer so – the heartache – it will be forever in my memory – never to be reconciled – I will have to pick a month – let me say October 1968 – it was time for the baby to be born – I believe it was Good Samaritan Hospital – things at this time period were most fragmented – I am making an effort to be as detailed as I can be – most of what happened from here on in – are flashes of time – continuity – will be in perspective – the haze that bordered me – encompassed my very being – I do not remember driving to the hospital – I was in the waiting room – the doctor came in – he said the baby was born – but died – it was a boy – he was deformed – he asked me "Do you want to see the baby" – I said – "No" – he left – I remember walking over to the hospital window – looking out into heavy gray rainy morning – the thoughts – are – will always be fresh - most clear - in my memory – for at this moment – I relived my whole life – the sadness in my heart – the immorality that swept my soul – the little boy walking up that hill – the tears of my lifetime – although not a tear was shed at this moment – the hate this women had for me – the visual of her pounding her unborn – the impartiality of life it self – the justice of God – this was provoked – the dark side of me prevailed – I could not escape the reality of what had taken place – the clandestine meetings - summoned at all hours of the night – that never took place – yet I had to go – with no destination – self-delusion – I pondered – but I would not give into it – I had a destination - I just did not know where – I do remember going into a mortuary – at which time a small coffin was picked out – the mortician – who was to pick the infant up at the hospital – buried the infant in an unmarked grave –as if it never existed – the advice from the doctor – I did not understand – maybe - to prevent the mother – myself – our children from mourning something that never was – but it was – it did exist – I also remember bringing no baby clothes to the hospital that morning – there was no ease in my being – wandered many a night – I stopped driving while drinking – I had been stopped over thirty-five times for drunk-driving – in the beginning it was fun – driving in those blackouts – thinking I was transported from Los Angeles to Fresno – no fun anymore – I had lost a lot of weight – January 1969 came - I was almost down for the count – I remember another episode that happened - my wife took off – I did not know where – she stayed away some days – but when I went upstairs – there were broken bottles – mirror – and ripped pictures – the room was torn apart – she was gone – I did fear for her – she left all the children – I made a promise – if she came home safely I would never drink again – how many times did I make that promise – I do remember forcing her to sign over twenty- one thousand dollars in stocks some years prior – my mind was going – there was no connection – from things that happened - and things that did not happen - she came home some time around eleven in the morning – I told her how sorry I was – for by this time my demeanor was not of a man – but a subservient human being – how many times did I say I would babysit if she would bring me home a bottle of gin – beer – wine – etc. or do the laundry for the same – I was not a father nor a husband – I was a shell – I remember meeting a barmaid in some bar - I strolled in – I shook for a drink – she gave it to me – she said I had a problem – she understood me – her name was Sally – she was a barmaid – she was just out of state prison - a five-year stretch – selling and possession of drugs – telling me I had a problem – so here it is eleven in the morning – with a promise never to drink again – we sat - we talked – I have no idea what we talked about – so many talks for so many years - I do remember this however – I was at the front door of our house - I looked at her and said – "I am going out to get a pack of cigarettes" – she gasped – "I have not been home three hours yet - and you're going out" – I told her "It will only be ten minutes" – three days later – I was in a blackout – woke up near Sacramento – my time was running out – the next few months starting January 1969 were most bleak – wandering in a daze of bewilderment – not knowing what day it was – reintroduced to Alcoholics Anonymous – same type meetings I went to sixteen years prior – the only difference being – I was going down for the count – I identified with all that was said – there was no way I could put anything together – I left each meeting waiting for the thunder and lighting – to be rendered sober – nothing ever happened – I kept on drinking – sometimes I would throw-up on myself – wake up in sordid places – no peace – the show was over – Alcoholics Anonymous did not work – I waited after each meeting for that thunder - that lighting to happen – but it never did – a man in the meeting hall named Bill Allison – told me I was going to die – the sores on my body were more prevalent – the internal bleeding more persistent – the weight loss most present – the obsession to drink – was constant – there was so much that left my thoughts that once were – nothingness prevailed – I truly wanted to die – the delirium tremens – I could not remember anything from one minute to the next – I could not talk to anyone – I could not hold a sentence together – nor hold a thought – I tried desperately to figure out where I was – what I was doing – where I was going – to no avail – January made it to February – March – April – May – I do not remember any thing that went on – I was alone in the truest sagacity – the intensity of the loneliness was crippling – bringing forth the day I made that long walk up the hill - to the orphanage - in the blinding snowstorm - with the tears running down my face – I lived a lifetime of emotions – so little joy – so much sadness – I had no place to go – I was saturated with alcohol – one of the last things I remember – might be in June of 1969 – I was driving a green '52 Chevy – somehow I saw those red lights behind me – I pulled over – the officer pulled in front of me – I got out – as did he – he had a shotgun pointed at me from behind his open door – it was two or three in the morning – I remember his words – "Don't move or I'll shoot you" I walked toward him – told him – to "shoot" – as I got close to him – and the shotgun – for some reason he put the gun up – told me to take it easy – started talking to me – I don't know what was said – he drove me home – I do not remember any continuity - in the next few weeks or months – a vague area of time - almost as though it did not exist – the empty caldron – filled with loneliness – there were no pictures - past or present – no beginning – no end – the next three episodes happened as I will describe – some time in June or the beginning of July - I do not know where or when these moments took place – nor how long they lasted – this is what happened - a warm –

encompassing – all-knowing feeling came over me – devoid of fear – paranoia – loneliness – only harmony – encompassed my being – with these feelings prevailing - the knowledge of my death was imminent – how long I was to live – I did not know – but for sure it was close – I don't know how much time elapsed from this one moment to this next moment that was about to be recalled – maybe days – sometime in the month of July - I came out of a blackout – was in Hollywood - in the middle of the street - directing traffic – I worked my way back to the empty house where I lived – I had a bottle of gin in my hand – leaned over the sink and uttered these words – "Please God help me – I don't want to drink this"- end of moment – what was about to happen is most vivid – a pulsating body – lights flashing in front of my eyes – I could scoop up the alcohol from the pores of my body – the stench intolerable – delirium tremens – phones that did not ring – but rang – the shaking – quivering - trembling – uncontrollable body – that rested – not by night - nor by day – the voices – that came from nowhere – the prevailing hopelessness – I did not eat – I felt so feeble – so weak - the internal bleeding – the sores on my body - all my thought processes gone – wondering what next was going to happen to me – this conduct continued for several days – there is one – only one thought that consumed me during this period of time – I wanted to drink with every fragment left of my being – obsessed – craving – shaking for the drink – the bottle was within my grasp – I tried desperately to drink from the bottle – to no avail – the bottle in my hand - would not go from my hand - to my mouth – I tried almost everything to drink during this episode – knowing it would help me – I could not conceive of what was happening to me – the fear I had of alcohol was unparalleled to anything I have ever experienced in my life – I wanted to drink so badly but could not – with all that was going on I did not understand the fear of drink – nor the incapability drinking the alcohol itself – I was lost somewhere in the sphere of extinction – a warm evening in August 1969 – I was walking to an Alcoholics Anonymous meeting – as I walked - my thoughts reflected as to what had happened – I tried desperately to comprehend – to no benefit – the one prominent – the only thought that was prevalent – was this – with my arms down to my side – I uttered these words – "I'm sober" – on I went – the people of Alcoholics Anonymous were most kind to me – I could not articulate words – in the meetings I would mumble – I knew nothing of what to say nor how to say it – my mind was washed of any fragments of knowledge – the thinking process was gone – I could not tell anyone of this deficiency – paranoia was most prevalent – I sat alone not being able to talk to anyone – trying to think where I was in this phase of life – depression to the extent I was unable to fathom the movement of my body – what was left of me was hopeless – most helpless – the sadness beyond anything that I have ever experienced prior – loneliness – the never-ending fear of drinking – I remembered that I was an actor – and yet I could not put a sentence together – I could not pronounce words – paralysis in my jaw – I remember putting marbles in my mouth – saying - kay key ki ko ku – ba be bi bo bu – etc. I was so embarrassed – here I was thirty–six years old – a fragment of a human being – the worth of myself – non-existent – stooped-over – scuffling along – I kept going to the meetings – waiting for that thunder to happen – this went on for several months – I was in an abandoned duplex in the hills of Hollywood – I had carton boxes for end tables – alongside of my mattress that I picked up on the street – I slept with a hatchet – I did not want any surprises – I had no money – I worked at odd meaningless jobs – when I went to an Alcoholics Anonymous meeting - I thought I had to have a wet drunk with me – (a wet drunk is someone who has not stopped drinking yet) - in order for the people at the meetings to let me in – so there I would be picking up drunks whereever I could find them – crazy – this is the way it was – this is the way it went – months passed – I put weight back on – showered shaved – little things - still could not talk too well – paranoia ever so present – most of my time was spent wondering how I would get back in the mainstream of life – I was so embarrassed – I would never tell anyone in Alcoholics Anonymous where I lived – reason being – I thought the people would not let me come back – I had this Big Book of AA that was given me from the start – I kept reading the first line of this chapter five – it went like this – "Rarely have we seen a person fail who has thoroughly followed our path"- I do not know how many times I read this line in the first

months of my sobriety – hundreds upon hundreds – and much more
- then one day I was reading it – suddenly I saw the words for the
very first time – I spoke softly – "Rarely have we seen a person fail
who has thoroughly followed our path"- the realization came to me –
if I would follow the path – which I did not know – I would not drink
– I could not wait 'til night came and off to a meeting I would go –
armed with information that no one had ever heard at these AA meetings – I was so excited – the meetings in 1970 were small - ten to fifteen people - 8:30 to 10 p.m. each night – coffee shops 'til 2 a.m. –
this night came - my turn to share – "Rarely have we seen a person
fail who has thoroughly followed our path"- all eyes went my way –
after months of mumbling – a clear sentence – I did make a slight
mistake though – I tried to put other sentences together – to no avail
– mumble – mumble – mumble – but I did end with " Rarely have we
seen a person fail who has thoroughly followed our path"- a small
piece – a fragment – a chip – was placed in my consciousness – it was
the first constructive thought I had in my head - in so very long a
time – the hopeless state I was in - was only beaconed by this one line
– every meeting I went to I started with this line – mumbled a little –
then ended with the line – I often wondered early on why no one ever
told me about this line – kept it to themselves for some reason I guess
– so here I was - a one-line genius – this went on for about three
months or so – then one night I came to the meeting with line two –
"our very lives as ex problem drinkers depends upon our constant
thought of others and how we can help meet their needs"- after the
meeting a guy named Don - came up to me outside and said -"Thank
God you turned the page" – I turned the page – life was still most
vague – the wonderment of what happened – never registered - I took
my children every two weeks – we went to the park and sat quietly –
getting to know each other was most hard – they would split a Coke
between the four of them – for that's all the money I had – I was
unable to talk to them – they knew something had taken place – I do
not think any of us knew – it was the fall of 1970 – time for me to
leave my duplex – I remembered the lost feeling I had – knowing this
time had arrived – a sense of loss – the simplistic form of existence
I was living – was about to change – I brought my mattress – a few

cardboard boxes – off I went to my new home – a ten by ten - one bath – one closet room – ninety-five dollars a month – I was really moving up – this is what I thought – always remembering the house I had in an exclusive area in Tarzana California – maybe this was my stepping stone to my new life – time passed – the growing process was slow – but it did proceed - it was 1972 I believe – March – I needed twenty-five dollars to pay my rent – I got a telephone call from someone asking me to paint the front of their garage – would I give them an estimate – over the phone I said twenty-five dollars – I knew I could pay my rent – he said yes – next day on the job – I had the garage opener in my hand – I went up the ladder to see if I could reach the top – I could – I pressed the opener inadvertently - the garage door started to open – I fell off the ladder - broke my ankle – I worked four hours on the broken ankle – I got my twenty-five dollars – by the end of the day my ankle was twice its size – laying in bed I got pneumonia – pleurisy – my attitude was so bad – I wanted to drink – I wanted to die – "Why have you forsaken me my God ?"- I was so hurt – so despondent – I felt so betrayed – I was alone again one more time – consumed with loneliness – I saw nothing but black- ness – the tears came to my eyes once again – I mourned for peace of mind – to no avail – I got a phone call – a man named Colin wanted to get sober – I had worked with so many people in this state – so off I went – with my bad attitude – pneumonia – and pleurisy – he was holed up in a place called The Sportsman Lodge – I told him he had to hold a bottle of gin in his hand - say these words – "Please God help me I don't want to drink this" he looked at me inquisitively - said "I don't drink gin" – I had no answer – he said he could make a decision – I learned something that day – I never again told people to hold that bottle of gin – the pains in my chest were excruciating – the pleurisy coupled with the pneumonia – handicapped with the cast on my ankle – made it impossible for me to step on the elevator – I col- lapsed in the hallway – could not move – could not talk – agonizing – unbearable – severe – pain - enveloped my being – I could not lift my arm up – there I lay – in the hallway - totally helpless – the para- medics came – I whispered to them it was not a heart attack – none the less off I went to the emergency room in a nearby hospital – while

I was on the gurney – the nurses shot me full of morphine to stop the pain – I went back to my room to recover – was there about a week – a knock on the door – it was the apartment managers – they told me that I had to leave due to the fact I didn't pay my rent – I remember them saying to me "You are welcome back when you get well" – so there I was helpless – it was so hard for me to believe I was in this situation – I never could understand the reasoning for these episodes – they were of no value to me – the discomfort of life was most prevalent – later on in this year a divorce was ensuing – I wound up with absolutely nothing – nothing from nothing leaves nothing – there I was alone – that feeling inside of me – the never ending mournful cry of despair – the inner soul – the prevailing unhappiness – this February 1973 I was to turn forty – my acting career was still moving – I worked – I also knew my talent was most deficient – I was not the same actor I was in 1964 or prior – the alcohol took a toll – I would always play the heavy – there was too much interference in my head - between the character and the situation – I was not free – I was saddled with fear – I tried with each show to improve – I just could not perform in the purest sense – I wandered from one apartment to another – reason being – I would run out of rent money – I kept hoping for that miracle to happen – the show that would change my life – my ankle that I broke a few years back was never set right – always swollen – much pain – I walked with a limp – the value of myself was non-existent – the situation with my children grew - this was most important – we now could go to a fast food place – each would get something to eat and drink – they would also come to my apartment every other week – we grew – 1974 – my former wife informed me she was moving back east with the children – this was an unprecedented blow - with far-reaching effect to my being – when I hung up the phone – I wept – I could not believe what was about to happen – the four children - and myself - grew together – from one shared Coke in the park – to sleepover's in my apartments that changed with the winds – I was talking in sentences by this time – not too much else – I was acting on television – I knew my talent was not even close to what it should be – there were many great actors I worked with past and present – this is what happened in the summer of 1974

– the four children sat with me in my apartment before going to the airport – as the time came close to leaving – we started to cry somewhat – we started our drive – quiet we were – we got to the airport – waiting at the terminal – sitting there – again not saying anything to each other – a silence – when it came time to board – we all looked at each other – we all started to cry – there was no holding back – the only scene I remember was watching them board the plane – tears on all our faces – as the door closed – I turned – could it be the same feelings my father had when he left me in that train station – the loneliness that encompassed me – that long walk back to the car – crying – five years the children and I grew together – my insides knew it was never going to be the same again – three thousand miles apart - is a long distance – so here I was forty-one years old – alone – that neverending emptiness – always moving from one apartment to another – I was always waiting for that one big break that would vault me into another dimension – never came - I had worked with hundreds of alcoholics and drug users by this time – I now lived in a one-room apartment over a garage – the many moves I made in 1970's - was on the phone many a night with someone in need – did many television shows – knowing full well my talent was not there - the first sign of self-worth came in 1976 – I realized I had been given the power to help others – up to this time I had been empty – no worth of self whatsoever – it was early 1977 - if I were to make any inroads on my talent I had to go back to a work shop – there was a friend of mine that was a marvelous director and acting coach – I knew Harry back in 1952 – I began arduously – for the next three years -relearning my craft – I began to get the purity of what I had as a young actor – I did more television shows – in 1980 I got a Charles Bukowski short film – in that same year I went to Florida to see my mother - who was in a hospital - most sick – she had heart problems – had a pacemaker - suffered from a severe stroke – sometime late in 1980 – I got a telephone call – my mother was not to be moved - yet Jack Mayo her husband – took her up in an airplane – she died over Baltimore of heart failure – yes I cried – I saw the years of agony – anguish – the painful life she lived – the sorrow she felt of my life – although we never brought it up – the thought of my early life only brought tears to her – I never blamed her for anything that ever happened to me – she loved me as no other mother loved her son – here she is dead – I never got to say – " Hey Ma I love you " or hold her hand before she died – or be with her at that last moment of life – I'm three thousand miles away – alone in one of my apartments – a whole lifetime came before me – the time she got into that car crash and almost died – she was with another man – I passed judgment – would not go to see her – the hundreds of pictures she took of me – the pride she had for me – the sports events she came to – football – basketball – swim meets – track – baseball – the meals she would make – the home she tried to make for me – the heartbreak she felt so many times – because of me – the financial help through the years – the love she had for her grandchildren – teaching me how to drive – she never relinquished her love for me – every year of my sobriety – I would give her a gold charm number representing each year of my sobriety – she would wear it with dignity - the tears came – the loneliness encompassed my being once more – I would never see her again - I now lived in a two-room apartment – I pondered why Jack Mayo took her up in the plane – knowing full well she should not be moved – as a few months passed I became aware that none of my mother's personal belongings came my way – her jewelry – personal mementos – pictures – she had boxes of pictures of me – my whole sports career – newspaper articles – etc. – her will – the money that she had – I pondered no more – Jack Mayo gave it all to his daughter – who told me all of my mother's jewelry was stolen at the airport – what a tragic ending – one of the few times I held a resentment – the incredulousness of what had taken place – so here I was one more time – holding the emptiness of life – sadness surrounding my being – the picture of her dying in that plane over Baltimore – the tears came – so did that resentment – I could not rid myself of those ill feelings I had for Jack Mayo – then one morning about thirteen months later - 1981 the fall – I got a telephone call from Jack Mayo – I started out saying you killed my mother – you betrayed everything that was morally and ethically right – you're a Judas – you sold me out - I unleashed verbiage from the vocabulary of indecency – far beyond my usage – the tears – the anger – the frustration – came flowing – I never stopped talking – I just kept going at him – I wanted to hurt him - as he had hurt me – I was the judge – I was the jury – I condemned him – my mother was dead – he is alive – there was a brief pause in this one-sided conversation – I heard a weak – muttered – voice on the other end – say – "and I'm paying for it now" – I said no more – for in this one instant – resentment fell – I was never to judge another human being from this moment forward – a powerful lesson learned – he died a horrible death - so his daughter said at the time of his passing – the realization came over me – he never got to enjoy my mother's fruits of her life – he never realized any joy – it did not bring my mother back – nor did I ever say he got what he deserved – he just did not exist – 1982 was here – my talent was honed – a job well done by my friend Harry – I had done that short Bukowski film – several other TV shows – it was so hard for me to believe it took all these years of toil to get my talent back to where it was in the late Fifties early Sixties – alcohol took so much from me – it was a rainy day sometime in the fall of this year – a Sunday to be exact – I picked up my son's dog Ben – he was most disheveled – a German Shepherd he is – we both were in the back of my truck – which had a camper shell on it – I got hamburgers for us both – we ate - looked at each other in a most knowing manner – somehow he was transmitting his feelings to me in a most profound way – somehow he became me - as that little boy - when I ran away from that second orphanage – when my grandfather picked me up in his arms - well Ben was saying the same words – "Please take me"- "Please take me"- I looked at him with wonderment in my eyes – I came close to him – I held him – I said "Nobody is going to take you any more" – the words my grandfather said to me in 1940 – except I was the grandfather and Ben was me – I cried in the back of that truck that evening – I held Ben ever so gently – he had a tough hard life – he was nine years old – alone many a day –many a night – he told me much that night – he was tired of running – tired of being alone – his life and mine ran parallel – the loneliness he felt - I felt – I could not believe all these emotions were coming from an animal – yet the communion between us was real – he was going to be my teacher – he was going to teach me the purest form of love – he was to give me wisdom beyond my years – instincts

– selflessness – I did not understand why I was to learn these principles – they were here – I was to learn – every job I did I took Ben
with me – I could feel his awareness of any given situation – before
I continue – I would like to state that in order for me to continue my
acting career – for the past twenty-eight years I worked at odd jobs to
support my career – a humbling experience – waiting – for that phone
to ring – my agent - with that one big break – every show I did – I
thought this was it – to no benefit – I always played the bad guy –
boring by this time – how close I came so many times – the heart-
break – the disappointments – the rejections – the alcoholism that
took every bit of talent I had within me – here I was again at that
point - 1983 – fifty years old – my talent back to where it was in the
late Fifties – before alcohol took hold – all the insecurities – fears –
worry – torments of not knowing my craft – vanished – twenty-one –
maybe twenty-two years lost – a lifetime that was never to be – but
was – living in a garage apartment – with my dog Ben – he was a
masterpiece of love – when I would touch him – the energy from his
soul would touch the inner of me – I would sense peace – an all-
knowing feeling would come over me – I took care of him as my
grandfather took care of me – we were alone – with each other – his
instincts became mine – his awareness became mine – long about the
tail end of this year beginning of 1984 – a young director wanted me
to do a short story by Bukowski – called The Man – his name was
Patrick Roth – the same director that directed me in the short
Bukowski film – he read me the short story over the phone – I did not
equivocate one second – I said yes – the range of this short story –
was the gamet of life – powerful – emotions beyond – funny – sad –
sadistic – above all - it was real – it was a two-character story – the
lady who played opposite me was a most talented actress – she would
bring everything needed to fulfill her character – this was going to be
performed once and only once – there was one catch – a very famous
director by the name of Danny Mann was to witness Patrick's work –
Danny Mann's work won an Oscar for best actress - Susan Hayward
– I Want to Live - Elizabeth Taylor –Butterfield Eight - Anna Mag-
nani –The Rose Tattoo - a Tony for Shirley Booth – Come Back Little Sheba – on Broadway – he was one of the elite directors in

Hollywood – all the pieces were in place – all the years of toil – disappointment – here was a body of work written by a very earthy man – a talented actress – and a man that had reached the depths of despair – yet no higher than the first step - that was reached many years ago – a plateau of loneliness – there was no drinking in the way – no fear – no ambivalence – my talent was pure – I was lucky enough to know what it was like to perform at the peak of my talent – both in New York – and Hollywood – the show went on that day – there was a great silence after the show – I left nothing behind – Danny Mann came forward – he called me sir – I remember – he asked me if it was real whisky that I was drinking in the play – I said "No" – was not enough – he went over took the bottle – smelled it – "You're right" he said - he went on to say he worked with many of the top stars in Hollywood – and Broadway – that he was never so frightened of what he saw - yet so moved – the lady I worked with was magnificent – it was one of those moments that come by – where the memory of what happened will last a lifetime – this day - this moment – I could be no better – Danny Mann was going to do a Broadway play – On The Waterfront – written by Budd Schulberg – I did What Makes Sammy Run – another Schulberg play - Danny asked me if I would like to play Pop Doyle on Broadway – my dream – my lifetime of loneliness – my lifetime of tears – came before me – I would be able to help so many people on the Bowery in New York – it was going to be exciting – several months passed by – I would speak to Danny many times – read with people – I could not believe - the aura of excitement - that came with this knowledge of what was about to take place – I was consumed with the prospect of how many people I could help – fall came – so did 1985 – Danny called me – the show was put on hold - indefinitely – they could not raise the money – alone again – the tears came – this time was different however – I had missed out on parts previously – somehow the desire to continue as an actor seemed so distant – I just did not have it in me to start over – I did several shows in 1985 – my heart was heavy – I was fifty-two years old – the splintered dreams lay at my feet – the hopelessness of my future – the sadness that consumed me – I had worked so very hard to redeem my talent – my instincts knew that this was my last chance to achieve anything – my career was over – there were no more tomorrows – no more waiting for my agent to call – no desire – no hope – no dream – thirty two years of chasing – chasing what – I did not even know now – what I was chasing – there was an emptiness - that sided with that lonely feeling - of that little boy walking up that hill - in the blinding snow storm – back in 1938 – I had my dog Ben – but only for a moment more – I held him in my arms as the doctor put the needle to his arm – life left him – I cried – I cried – I cried so much – my heart broken – my heart so full of sadness - my heart so wounded – I wanted so - to die – I cried for days – the orphanage came back – the years of loneliness surfaced – lingered – I wanted to drink after sixteen years – he taught me so very much – I was in his soul – he was in mine – the communion between me and the animal kingdom was ever so prevalent – I will always hold him in my arms – he will remain forever in me – 'til the day I join him – of all the broken dreams – lonely days – sad moments – tears – this day – will be forever embedded in my soul – I learned this day - that the only thing that separates dog from human – is the intellect of man – the heart cannot make the separation – the loss is the loss – the terrific pain that accompanies the loss of something that will never come back – is far reaching – never ending sorrow – can never be justified – rationalized – in any form whatsoever – it just is – the emptiness that will accompany my being from this moment on – will join the myriad of lonely feelings that have encompassed my life thus far – it was this year 1985 that I changed my name – I took my grandfather's last name – Castellani – Raymond J. Castellani – was to be my handle for the rest of my life – I changed everything I could – I wanted no remembrance of my prior name – every time I mentioned my name – I got a warm feeling – my grandfather's arms were around me at all times – this was good – I never called any of the studios about my name change – I knew my career was coming to an end – 1986 was here – I was sitting in a movie theatre – Mississippi Burning was on the screen – the opening scene was one black boy accompanied by a white boy riding in the back seat of a car – they were murdered – I flashed back to 1954 – Singleton and myself in that bar Jacksonville Florida – I was ready to take on six guys –

here it was 1986 – it was my first realization of what could have happened that day – Singleton – myself – could have taken a ride – never
to be remembered – this was before Martin Luther King – I truly
believed in equality then – I am coming into focus at this juncture of
my life now - I do not know exactly what it is – at fifty-three – it was
early on in 1986 – I was working on an inlaid table – normal as can
be – when suddenly a feeling came over me – most acute – there were
no words – no visions – it was a powerful – I must say a most powerful placement of an idea - imbedded in my consciousness – I could
not escape the awareness that was present – I stopped what I was
doing – the message – loud and most clear - I was to clean up every
malfunction used to deceive – every lie – every dishonest thought –
every thought of self – every thought of succeeding – I was to put
forth - four words – purity – honesty – unselfishness – love – incom-
prehensible – there was no way I could incorporate these ideas in my
life – so far out of reach – was this the power of God – is this His
vision – I questioned – it was so profoundly succinct – or was this my
mind playing a game – self-deceiving thoughts - I tried to flush these
thoughts out – to no avail – they prevailed - these four words – on the
surface I knew what they projected – to incorporate them in my life
- is another matter - a sullen feeling came over me – here I was again
- alone – how alone – displaced from life itself – my dog Ben gone –
my career – this overpowering – overwhelming – cleansing idea – to
be integrated in my being – my mind bounced from every episode
encompassing my life – I tried so hard to figure out what my next
move was to be – but nothing came – my garage apartment was being
sold – I should say the property – so here I pondered – I pondered
purity – I pondered honesty – I pondered unselfishness – I pondered
love – they were words only to me - the next several weeks would
shed light on these ideas – I could not escape the onslaught – the
power – the driving force that propelled me to incorporate these four
ideas in my being – for what purpose – the infidelities of my life surfaced – the crooked paths – the oblique thoughts for so many years –
the double standards that masked my very being – purity was a word
I never realized existed in conjunction with the human mind – at least
in my mind – it was foreign to me – I kept going over the word purity

– there can be no outside object whatsoever to cast a shadow on this word - purity – it must stand alone – any intruding fragment would contaminate the entity – the mind – the body – the very soul of self – must implement the worthiness of purity – I cannot believe all this knowledge - of a few words - was transmitted to me – yet here it is – purity laid at my side – I was to start with the clarity – uncompromised – growth of purity – I guess I only touched the surface of this word – time will tell – here came honesty – as if I did not have enough going on with purity - honesty must prevail – every thought in my consciousness – every thought in my subconscious psyche must be put to the test - of honest reality – there can be no deviating from honesty – no words from my mouth can ever be slanted – or misconstrued with deception – this will be the working part of my mind – again I questioned – why – for what purpose – no answer – honesty will be weighed by each thought from me - from here on in – I will become a black and white person – there will be no gray areas – only the fullness of honesty – it is not to be used as a hammer to hurt anything or anyone – to be harmful in any way – the eyes must reflect the inner self of truth – next in this avalanche of awareness - came unselfishness – this came most rapidly – there can be no thought of self whatsoever – in any form – it came down just like that – the last of these ideas was love – I did not understand why love was one of the ideas – it seemed to be self-explanatory – nonetheless here I stood with these four concepts – there was no way I could elude them – so toward the end of 1986 I had made slight inroads on this sort of thinking – it was power-driven - by a force much greater than myself – there was no escaping – still no reason why I had to incorporate these four entities into my life – I got most despondent during this period of time – there seemed so little for me to do in life – no more furniture-making – no more desire to work – no career – no women to care for - and too - to care fore me – Alcoholics Anonymous – was but a shell of what it was in 1969 – it also was instilled in me to - do no more sharing at the meetings – so here I was with seventeen years of sobriety – to keep my mouth shut – I felt so lost – no direction whatsoever – a strange thought came to me – again – powered by a source – it was clear - I was to relinquish all connections in Los Angeles – sever all ties – apartment – bank accounts – people – agent – any connection to what was left of my acting career – I was to stand alone – not knowing where I was going – or what I was to do – I had my white truck with the camper shell – I got a small bed roll – outfitted the back of my camper – with no place to go – or any idea where to go – the only thoughts in my mind were these four ideas – purity – honesty – unselfishness – love – I got in my truck and off I went – every dream – every hope of success – every person I knew – every horrid experience – the small triumphs – the yes's – the no's - the heart breaks – the toils of a lifetime – the tears – the smiles that were so few – are a memory at this juncture of my life – the loneliness that accompanies my being at this time – parallels - that of me being dropped off at that orphanage in 1937 – I keep going back to this episode of my life – I cannot outrun these feelings - the wonderment of nothingness – I can't explain it – empty – tears came to me – I would sleep in the camper at night – have bologna sandwiches – move on – every day I would ask for guidance from the power of God – to no gain – abandonment – the days turned into weeks – the tears I shed every day – the flashbacks of many of the happenings in my life – the multitude of mistakes that I had made – the misconducts – the untruthful manner of my being – haunting – there was no peace – just tears - loneliness - many times I would pound my dashboard – pleading to God for guidance – each time - a vacuum – the rain – the cold – the constant driving – going no where – there was no understanding of what was happening to me – if anything was happening to me – I was that little boy again – only this time there was no grandfather to pick me up – to hold me in his powerful arms – to give me courage – to give me his warmth – to secure my soul – I pleaded to God to shed some light – the weeks became months – anger - frustration - were setting in – it was hard for me to fathom why all this was going on – nothing was being accomplished – no awarenesses – no knowledge of enlightenment – tears – loneliness – I don't remember now how many months I was driving – nor how many towns I went through – thoughts would begin to come in my head – one day feelings were most prevalent – to take right turns or left – out of this anger and frustration – every thought that came to me as to where to go – I went the opposite way – I was going to show God – I was in control – I felt so good that night – that I checked into a motel – I decided to go to an AA meeting – it was a small town – I called information – got a call in to someone – found out that there was a meeting two blocks away – I did think it was a little strange – after me going all day long the opposite way I was directed to go – I wind up two blocks away from an AA meeting – nonetheless off I went – as I approached the door going in – the man at the door greeted me – asked me if I would be the speaker of the group this night – I said "No thank you" – went in - sat down – waited for the meeting to begin – a few minutes passed by - the gentleman came up to me again - asked if I would speak – this time I said – "Yes" – most reluctantly - now I shared this night – people came up to me after the meeting – they had tears in their eyes – the accolades that night - were most prevalent – the people were hungry for what I had to say – I do not remember anything of what I said – whatsoever - that night – a strange feeling came over me when I left the meeting – all day long I thought I was doing everything my way – every direction – every turn – was opposite of where I thought He would have me go – yet I wound up in some small town – talking to a group of people – saying what He wanted me to say to them – it was His direction – His party - His show – I had no control – even though I thought I did – I went back to the motel – the only thought in my head was – maybe I am being directed – I just did not know - next day the same unknowing feeling – I got in my white truck – off I went to nowhere – I have been on the road seven months or so – 1987 winter – spring – summer - now fall – where was I to go – I was close to the Oregon border one day – I would say late September – to recap this trip in a few short phrases – is most easy – I went nowhere – extreme loneliness – tears every day – no understanding of what was going on – bewilderment – frustration – anger – all the time asking for the Will of God – pounding that dashboard of my truck – to no benefit – so here I am - near the Oregon border – a thought came into my mind – a very powerful – straight forward – no frills – I want you to go back to Los Angeles – I could not believe the feeling – it consumed my being – the direction was so strong – no other thought entered my mind – I stopped the truck – pulled over to the side of the road – I sat – I pondered – incredulous – could this be what I was asking for – or was my mind playing tricks on me – I had no peace of any sort – these past months – no relief of the agony – anguish - suffering – in this stretch of time – I checked into a motel that night – I left Los Angeles months before – never to return I thought – so here I was - a strong – most powerful feeling – to go back to Los Angeles – what was I to do there – was the question – was I to wander in this maze of nothing – go back to Alcoholic Anonymous – where I did not fit – go back to acting – a career that ended before I realized it – I had no place to live – it had been eighteen years since I lost the home I once owned – I had very little money – I could not remove myself from that overpowering feeling to go back to Los Angeles – in the morning I started to go north toward the Oregon border – I must have been thirty or forty miles away from reaching Oregon – I stopped my truck – pulled over – the feelings were such – I could no longer go forward – I sat – I do not know how long – I realized I no longer had a choice – I must turn this truck around and be on my way back to Los Angeles – this is exactly what I did – a strange peace came over me – it seemed like there was no fight left in me – those four ideas kept infiltrating into my mind – purity – honesty – unselfishness – love – there was to be no deviating from this format – I must incorporate these entities to the fullest - in my being – again no choice – it must be done now – was the powerful feeling that encompassed me – there was no escape – no procrastination – the destination was Los Angeles – what I was to do there - was the ambiguity – the uncertainty – the vagueness - nonetheless I drove south – I was obedient to the direction – I got to Thousand Oaks – still no direction on what I was to do – so I stayed in Thousand Oaks for about a month – I was well into November 1987 – each day seeking the knowledge of His Will as to what my next move was to be – nothing came – this whole tormented – lonely - forlorn journey – was it to end up on a blank page of my life – another alley of loneliness filled with tears – I was fifty-four years of age – sitting on nothing – waiting for direction – from a power called God – with these four ideas of purity – honesty – unselfishness – love - if I told anyone this story – I know what they would say – maybe I was a little crazy – life had taken everything from me – most of all desire – desire to do anything – desire to achieve anything – every dream I ever had was unlived – I got this direction to come back to Los Angeles – I did - here I am stripped of any dignity – waiting for some sign as to what to do – I was in a total – complete – self-contained – vacuum – the aloneness was all consuming – so I waited – I think a week or so went by – it was toward the end of November 1987 – those ideas of – purity – honesty - unselfishness – love – were towering thoughts – the only thoughts – that were foremost in my mind – the uneasiness that accompanied my being for the past several years – the trip for the past nine months – the sadness that persisted – the aloneness – it seemed would only be my persona from now on – another driving force came into my being at this time – it was one of the most oblique – disconcerting – unfathomable enigmas – that came to me – in this trying time of my life – this was the direction laid out for me – I had been on many a Skid Row while I was drinking – had gone to AA meetings on Skid Row years before – to recapture the truth of AA – to no avail – had worked with hundreds most likely thousands of addicts – alcoholics – many trips to hospitals – was schooled for eighteen years – in drugs and alcohol – and now - I was to go down to Skid Row with food – pass it out – that was it – no other information – no other direction - just that – I could not disconnect from this direct feeling – the power to fulfill this quest – was overpowering – much to my dismay – I asked for His guidance – I pleaded – I begged – I cried – now this – Skid Row was not even remotely connected to what I imagined myself to entertain – it was incredulous for me to pursue such an endeavor – I baulked – I baulked – I baulked – at the same time – overpowered - by the feeling as to what I was directed to do – there was no escape – came December 1987 – where was I to get the food – money – what was I to serve – nothing – nothing – an empty vat – December first or second – a direction ensued – which I followed – that being to go back to the church – which in 1974 I brought the first AA meeting to — I was not foreign to the secretary nor to the pastor – so on this day in December – I went into the office – I also realized – if I got enough no's – I would not have to fulfill the direction given to me – how well

I remember this morning – I walked in - sat down – I knew Becky - the secretary - from previous years – I felt really out of place – I knew I was going to ask her for the use of the kitchen for Saturday – I was to tell her it was to feed some people - so I asked her – she came back at me with a question – what location was I to feed these people – I took a deep breath – I knew at this moment she was going to think I was crazy – I said Skid Row - downtown Los Angeles – I was not going to tell her I was following direction from the Master Himself – I knew she would think at that moment I was crazy – I was waiting for a no – she pondered for a moment – opened the desk drawer – pulled out a key – it was the key to the kitchen – I can't say I was thrilled – I did take it – the next question she asked – what are you going to serve – I had no answer – a women came through the office door – Becky told her what I was going to do – she immediately said I could get bread from across the street – so here I was – I had a kitchen – I had bread – some one gave me peanut butter – also jelly - it was December fifth 1987 – three a.m. – it was cold – it was rain- ing – I made one hundred eleven peanut butter and jelly sandwiches that morning – I waited for dawn – I had two friends of mine that met me at eight a.m. – off we went to Skid Row – what happened next was a moment in my life that was most profound – I passed out the sandwiches to the broken souls of our society – it took about three minutes – the rush for the food - the area reeked of anguish – the aroma of urine – the cleansed feelings of despair – the energy that any second something may erupt – not to the good – the cold – the dampness – that shed from their bodies – the hopelessness on the faces - of so many – the dried blood around their lips – around their eyes – ninety-five percent black – what a statement – this is Skid Row – downtown Los Angeles 1987 - a feeling came over me that impacted my innermost self – I felt at that instant - I touched the soul of mankind – I followed the direction of the Master – it took me to the bottom of our society – where death is imminent for so many – where murder is an every day occurrence – where rape lurks in the alleys – I fulfilled the directions that were given – Sunday came – Monday – I could not elude the feelings that persisted – that being to go back downtown this coming Saturday – I so did not want to go –

I had no place to live – no job – no money – just these four ideas of purity – honesty – unselfishness – love – along with this driving force to go back downtown on Saturday – there was a call from my answering service that Universal Studios wanted me for a show – I waited 'til Friday to call them back – sure enough it was me they wanted – Simon and Simon was the show – I was guaranteed – separate plate at the top of the show – I made six thousand dollars that week – the most I ever made in all the years of acting – some how it just did not do it for me – the pain of my whole career - was forever present – the preceding thirty-two years was too vast of an episode of my life to be traded in for the hope of tomorrow – what could be – what might be – will not be – nonetheless the week between Christmas and New Year I was to do the show – overpowered I was with this feeling to go back downtown – December twelve 1988 - yes the food showed up – down I went with my son Raymond – the onslaught of humanity was something to behold – the energy was beyond anything I have ever witnessed – there was no fear in my being whatsoever – I got a sliver of a glimpse - what purity stood for – I had no agenda – I had no ulterior motive – I just wanted to give the food with no strings – somehow the people of the streets picked up on this – I served one hundred and eleven sandwiches the first week – this week maybe one hundred and twenty or so – I kept track for some reason – the next week I picked up some volunteers – back downtown I went – I somehow could not get away from the overwhelming feeling to repeat the next few weeks in the same manner as the previous week – January 1988 – volunteers came – more food showed up – downtown - a line was waiting for me each week – by the end of January the line numbered in the hundreds – as each person passed me – I handed them food – I looked them poignantly in the eye – crowding out any doubt one might think I was false – a strange power was coming forth – I could feel the connection – it was certainly not manufactured by me – the word purity kept surfacing – I realized I was doing something I had no control over – everything was being done fore me – I was just following His directions – people worked side by side with me – many people stepped up – the latter part of 1988 we became a foundation - a 501-C3 – Frontline Foundation - could this be what I was destined to do – by the end of 1988 over forty thousand meals had been served – I could not believe the number – I knew the power of His Will was being executed – the food was always present – donors would surface – it was His show – I was just the care taker – I became aware that I was to trust this entity – this source of energy – the power that was instilled in me - through Him – never to deviate or digress - from His Grace – I must encompass – put into practical application – compassion – understanding – tolerance – to put His wisdom through me to others – I began to see all people as equal – never to separate the flock – only to see His children – I began truly to fathom - purity – one of those four ideas given to me some years back – to see – hear – sense – the depth by which this word represents – the clarity – there can be no interference of any sort whatsoever – it cannot be contaminated by any justifications – rationalizations – the word purity – stands alone – never to be compromised – this is what I must live by – the position I am in allows me to feel pain – as I have never felt before – never to be governed by my pain - allows me to feel someone else's joy – I have been given insight to feel the emotions of others – to give of myself – the aloneness that accompanies this terrain - is most forlorn – I have come to realize that the food I bring downtown is most irrelevant – it is the caring – it is the touch – it is in the eyes – by the end of 1990 over one hundred and eighty thousand meals have been served – a happening beyond anything I ever expected – the unfolding of a great miracle – to think that one hundred eleven peanut butter and jelly sandwiches started this avalanche – the unwanted souls of Skid Row – the discarded – the despondent – the deranged minds of some – the alcohol drenched bodies – the drug-infested minds that wander the streets for another fix – or a crack pipe waiting – or just a soul waiting to die – these are the children of the Master – I feel all this array of torment – I keep following His dictates – the incorporation of the second of these ideas that were given to me some years ago has also been prominent these past few years – honesty – I found myself never faltering on this word – trueness - became prevalent – there were no more lies – no more fabricated stories – just truth – the people of the streets – have been lied to – misled – misrepresented – harassed – deprived –

above all – treated without dignity – these are His children – I am my brother's keeper – I realize this more and more – as I shed the skin of self – I now call these ideas – principles – purity – honesty – unselfishness – love – they now have become paramount in my being – these principles will guide me for the rest of my life – unselfishness is a beautiful - most revealing - entity of one self – there can be no thought of self whatsoever – it stands alone – 1992 I strayed from trust – I thought I was to work to get money to pay my rent – I got a hot dog cart – started selling dogs to make a living – in the meantime Frontline was going broke – during this time frame - I received a commendation from President Bush – but something most powerful was about to take place – the awareness came over me that I did not trust in the power of God – when I found out about Frontline's financial problem – I realized my mistake – if I was to trust the power to run the show – it must be the whole show – I must turn all of me over to Him - I remember going to the kitchen one evening – a group of church people were going to buy Frontline for the amount I owed – five thousands dollars was the debt – it was in a white envelope – I was sitting down – they put the envelope in front of me – all I had to do was take it – financial problem would be solved – I asked them if they would give me a week to think it over – the direction was there – I had no choice – next day a man came up to me while at the stand with fourteen hundred dollars – two days later J C Penny donated Frontline three thousands dollars - that Friday a man came up to me and wanted to buy the hot dog cart – the price was right – I went back to the kitchen – I was only directed to feed the people – nothing else – this is where I strayed – I must be obedient to His calling – I must never stray from His dictates – I realized then I became His servant – the path is most arduous – the strain – three more years passed – over four hundred thousand meals served – incredulous - 1995 I was awarded the President's Service Award – considered the nation's highest volunteer award – I stood in the Rose Garden of the White House – was presented the award by President Clinton – he thanked me for taking care of the people of Skid Row – Los Angeles – I answered back – "Thank you Mr. President – for the better part of thirty-two years I sought a career – wanted to make it to the top of the ladder – pursued each and every road that was in front of me – that would enhance my career – weathered all storms of disappointment – lied – cheated – morally wounded – put four principles in my life – fed a few people - here I am in the Rose Garden with the most powerful man in the world" – tears came to my eyes – I was here on behalf of the people of Skid Row – it is their award – 1995 approaching half a million meals served – many of the people of the streets were elated – saying we made it to the White House – I have done many interviews - radio – television – many articles in magazines - newspapers – the lessons I have to learn – trust the power of God – times were hard – my heart was not good – money was short – lost my hospitalization – I did go to the VA – just keep feeding the people - so I did – I did marry again – she worked with me side by side – she got a few dogs - Priscilla – Samantha – Sonny Boy –I love them so – the pain of Ben was still with me – more so now – the purity vested in me – could no longer ease pain from the reality of what is – I knew the head made the distinction between human and animal – the heart knows no such distinction – it just plain hurt – the tears for the loss of Ben – the wrenching agony in the hollow of my being will forever be – here I am again – with those four principles – Purity – Honesty – Unselfishness – Love – the last of which is love – somehow this word is tossed around like a cork in a mild ocean – trying to seat somewhere – where prevails - Purity – Honesty – Unselfishness – I understood these past years what the last of these principles stood for - Love – I love purely – I love honestly – I love unselfishly – without one thought of self – this way of life is not easy to live with – loneliness is most prevalent – the animals live this way – if they are not tampered with by humans – the wild animals in the jungles care for their offspring – in this manner – thus is the power of these four words – I know why these principles were given to me – the thousands of people these past years that I confronted – with only a second to react at times – had to convey power – without brawn – understanding - without conflict – tolerance - without weakness – had to love Purely – Honestly – without one thought of self – the feelings of loneliness that have been with me my life – remain – they are part of my make up – the deep understanding I have for humanity –

prevails because of this loneliness – compassion - prevails because of this loneliness – I feel acutely - happenings – example being - several years ago a young women drove two of her children into a lake – she got out – the two children did not – I feel the horror of those two children – their last moments – "What is happening mom" – they cried out – with fear in their little hearts – not understanding what was going on – as the water crept up – their little hands grasped at the windows – I believe God intervened – purity is harsh at times – whenever I reflect on this tragedy – I weep – a great sadness comes over me – I felt this sadness many times in my life – as I have grown older – freer of self – the compassion for others becomes paramount – the deeper the concern for others – there is so little I know – knowledge seems to be slipping away – supplanted by simple ideas of life – the realization of a half million meals – never comes to the forefront – I lost just about everything I had – the struggle – the arduousness of following His direction is hard for me to comprehend – I only knew one thing – feed the people – not food – compassion – honesty – tolerance – to listen to what each had to say – understanding – to touch – the broken – the forgotten – downtrodden souls laden with alcohol – those too in that world of drugs – I felt so at ease in this environment – the Master Himself – revealed the knowledge of how to handle each and every situation – each and every person that came to the forefront – it was not me that handled these thousands of soul - of humanity - every week – I was just the instrument used – it is His miracle – I just followed His directions – the end of each year brought more numbers – by the end of 1998 over six hundred thousand meals were served – I remember back so many times to that trip I took in 1987 – begging for direction – I cannot believe eleven years have passed – Purity – Honesty – Unselfishness – Love – prevail – the emptying out of all pre-knowledge – conceptions – ideas – the incorporating of these four principles – this is all that I was left with – I had to exemplify – demonstrate – these principles – there was nowhere for me to turn – I only had this one direction – lonely again – only this time I had direction – so on I went – realizations came to these past years – it was not important to be first – not important to be the best – not important to know the answers - I could not understand these thoughts that came into my head – a leveling of self – to be able to listen – I was a tyro – everything I needed came to me – there was nothing to prove – almost like I was playing ball in a vacant lot - all by myself – I could not explain this chapter of my life to anyone – in the year 2001 over seven hundred thousand meals will have been surpassed – I take no credit for this happening – there is just a flat line in my being – philosophy of life in a different form - began to infiltrate in my life – equality among mankind – became most prevalent – the realization of how many years passed by since my birth – I began to become cognizant of the fact that I have run the race of life – and came in last – a very comfortable feeling came over me – hard to explain – yet so true – all my life wanted to be the best at what I did - or do – here I stand almost seventy years old – at ease finishing last in the race of life – most prevalent was - the idea of being a servant - of - for the Master – I felt so frail – so unworthy to this calling – yet the power of His entity – so prevailed – His wisdom guided me – words came to me that would help others – the touch of me - to my fellows – by word – or action - I was never to preach – never to stand apart from – I was never to want for anything – I was to rely on Him for everything – every thought – every emotion – every breath I took – by the year 2005 over eight hundred thousand meals have been served on the streets of Skid Row – a miracle – His miracle – there was one man I was talking to about this phenomena – dear friend Craig – we would converse hours at a time - days – and too - as the years rolled on – this miracle was not confined to Skid Row – thousands of young people crossed over the threshold to Frontline's kitchen – giving for the purity of giving – people well on - in their later life - came to give – middle aged – so many – on and on – the mailing list afforded the opportunity for people to support from afar – it was again directed to me to thank each person straightforwardly – that being a hand-written note – His vision to be carried via these notes – 2006 came – the spring – divorce ensued – a change of heart – no chance of reconciliation – much to my dismay – I cried so much – for what could have been – never became – my heart most heavy – the tears never stopped – the loneliness at this stage of my life – I could not fathom – I reiterated hundreds of times a day – "I am Your servant my God" – I arduously went through each day – with the business at hand – she bombarded everyday with scenarios as to - where to live – how to live – how am I going to pay for this – or that – on and on – with no stop – every word from her mouth – pierced my heart – she went to England – she had absolutely no consideration for me – I trusted the power of God – with the tears flowing – I questioned the principles – purity – honesty – unselfishness – love – I wanted to make sure I was on the right path these past eighteen years – so I looked them up on the internet – what I found – most profound – I had inverted the first two of these principles - honesty came before purity – it went like this – Honesty – Purity – Unselfishness – Love – these were given to me some eighteen years ago – for me to incorporate in my being – to live by them – never to deviate – to comprehend them – I needed the power coming from these principles – to offset energy exuded by the onslaught of humanity I was facing each day on Skid Row – but here I was wounded – weakened – destabilized – am I on the right path – so through the tears – here is what came to me – these principles are called the Four Absolutes – given to Jesus by the Master – to use these principles for the lessons of mankind – Jesus gave them to John – Matthew – and Luke – if these Four Absolutes are good enough for the Master – to give to Jesus – to give to the disciples – they are good enough for me – from now on I will call them Four Absolutes – I will say them in their right order – a reconfirmation of what was given to me eighteen years ago – I have incorporated these Four Absolutes in my life – not knowing what the significance held – nor the origin – but I know now the reason they were given to me – to give me the power – to give me strength - the fortitude - the courage – to fulfill the conditions of the Master – for eighteen years – I have sought His Will – believing every moment that I was guided – that over 850,000 meals were served – as a result of His Will – but more important was His vision – of compassion – of understanding – of tolerance – of one soul touching another – of talking the language of the heart – of being His instrument – of feeling His power flow through me - to His flock – of caring – the arduous – arduous – road – these past eighteen years – the sicknesses that I have endured – the never ending pounding of wants from the people of the streets on Skid Row – my lessons of being His instrument – came hard – most costly – Purity – the second of these Absolutes – total – complete - surrender to His Will – not one fragment – not one thought – not one oblique idea – must come between His Will and myself – purity has no wants – no desires – these are human traits – which I have – but give no credence to – my feelings are my feelings – they will never stand in the path of what His Will is for me - these months pass – but I cannot disregard the intense grief – anguish is nothing new for me – I lost my Priscilla girl – I lost my Samantha – I lost Buster – I lost my beautiful boy - Sonny Boy – the pain of losing these animals has marked me for the rest of my living days – along with my Ben – they surface each day – of every day of my life – tears are shed – the agony of the losses – the loneliness that encompasses the memory of each – I cry – I cry – I never want to outrun the anguish - that the remembrance of these God-given creatures – presents – a few years after Ben died – a vision came to me – maybe in a dream – or the twilight of waking up – a long dark corridor – round I would say – at the end was an ever-so-bright light – luminous in nature – most brilliant – there in the center sat Ben – the magnificent nature of his being – so defined – so pure – so radiant – waiting – waiting for me – my heart is heavy - will always remain heavy – the tears will always be – the loneliness will always be – 'til that day comes when I walk through that corridor – the glory of being with Ben – accompanied by Priscilla – Samantha – Buster – Sonny Boy – my grandfather – my godfather – without question - of course - the Master Himself – this does not ease the pain – it only accompanies the pain – maybe it is time for me to end this walk of life – I have traveled that long lonesome road – I have missed many opportunities in my life – if any of them became a reality – would I be where I am today – would I think the way I think – would I believe how I believe – would the Master be my center - what is my final destination – there are no more mountains for me to climb – no more valleys for me to pull myself out of – I have truly run the race of life – I have come in last – I see everyone in front of me - scampering – for that number-one spot – as I did for so many years - the vision of life has laid itself before me – not how much I have gained

- in wealth – or in fame – or how many - boats – cars – planes – or how many houses I have – it is in the understanding of a fragmented soul - on the verboten streets of our society – it is in the understanding of the whole of humanity – not to discard any - I have nothing to prove any more – just be myself – for the sake of being myself – I answer to only one source – the Master – His watchful guidance – carried me through a lifetime – all the why's – all the how's – all the doubts – all the turns – all the downfalls – all the limited highs – all the multitude of mistakes – He guided me to the full reality of self-lessness – to the reality of caring for my fellow beings – He guided me to the true reality of compassion – understanding – He guided me only to rely on - His direction – He has given me power – to be used only - to help others – with all this guided – magnificent display of His presence – I am still a human – I do follow the principles – the Four Absolutes – following these principles allows me to fulfill His will – but under no circumstances – am I exonerated from feelings – feelings of aloneness – feelings of sadness – tears come to me when I think of my lost animals – tears come to me when I feel my grand-father's arms holding me – as I cried for him to take me - tears come to me when I think of my father – the last time I saw him in that train station – when he boarded that train by himself – knowing he was never going to see his son again – tears come when the imagery of that beautiful Japanese girl sat on the edge of the bed – with tears running from her eyes – the last words I will always hear over and over – her soft voice saying – I never see you again – me saying – no – her saying – Sayonara – me saying the same – closing the bamboo sliding door - on a memory - that has lasted my lifetime – when purity is present – reality surfaces – there will be no justifications – nor rationalizations – nor will I compromise purity - I feel what I feel – I am human – with emotions – I have no fear whatsoever – because of the principle of Purity – feelings are accented – emotions are accented – awarenesses are most vivid – I feel with great intensity my fellow beings – it is for me to understand the ones who can't be understood – it is for me to present care – not through the word of hope – but through the action of touch – to continually give for the purity of giving – never to want anything in return – it is through the nothingness in my being – that I have been given the grace – the knowledge - to help others in some small way – I realize full well - as I stand on the threshold - of a million meals served to humanity – I only followed the directions from the Master – truly nothing I have done – I am humbled – truly humbled – the effort from so many – as I look back over my life – as I approach the end of my life – I am cognizant of the fact that I have done little to enhance our world – the principles that are at hand in my life form - are principles that can change the outlook of any society – in one moment – yet they are estranged to most – they lay dormant – the struggle of living – life – death – goes on – a blink of an eye – twenty years will have passed – generations – then a century – wars – earthquakes – hurricanes – tornados – tsunamis – etc. etc. prevail in this blink – then history – in the framework of eternity – which is measured by a humming bird's beak - to be sharpened - once every two thousand years – on a block of granite – standing one hundred miles high – one hundred miles wide – one hundred miles deep – when this cube of granite is rendered to dust – one day of eternity has passed – can I measure eternity in a day – no - so the moment is now – this moment I must awaken these estranged principles – I must awaken these dormant principles – I must put forth an effort to incorporate them in my life – so for twenty years plus - I have digested these four principles – most simple – most direct – most profound – they have given me - the wisdom – the power – to carry forth His direction – I have been obedient to His calling – the price has been dear – the emptiness that presides within my frame – has been – and is – a part of my existence – I believe now – true peace will be achieved when I take that final step - into His Kingdom – I have no problem feeling what I feel – I never want anything more – I do wonder sometimes – if that Broadway play became a reality – if drinking did not render me immobile for so long – draining me of my very life itself – instead of losing my talent – I would have been a part of – would things be different with my first love – Bobbie De Maria – had I been stable – not wanting to visit the world – she loved me so – I for her – I was so busy wanting to be everywhere – sensing – experiencing – life itself – I had no time to waste – on little things – like love - here I am in the twilight of my life

– I ponder – what would have been – it is hard to believe that after fifty-four years of life – feelings are generated with great passion - with great love – for her – she was so kind – so compassionate – so selfless - I believe so well – a partner comes by - once – maybe twice – in a lifetime – where the yokes are even – at the beginning of - at the end of – I have been fortunate to have touched it - twice – I have been unfortunate - twice – for they are only a memory – a memory of - that glow – a memory of - wanting to be with that one person – the scent – the touch – the singleness of each – consumed with feelings for each other – they are a memory – she never grew old – for I have never seen her – from that time to present – a lifetime – I do not know what the odds are – for a third time – but I do know this – if it does – whatever life is left in my being – roses will be laid at the feet of – columns of purity – selflessness – will uphold the standard of love – with all the passion – with all the glory – vested in me – if God shall choose – there are a multitude of past happenings that could have changed destiny on my behalf – had I chose a different path – so I am here in the present – with memories – memories of a child dying at birth – not giving that child a birth stone or place – a beautiful women found dead – after three days with her dog still by her side – I tried so to help her so many times – to no avail - a young women with so many suicide attempts – her arm looked like a wash board – I felt the wounds – I felt her pain - what could I have done or said to change her destiny – she completed – or a man – Tom Arnell – I still remember his name – saying to me one night – 1973 or so – how lucky I am to have life so simple – I still remember putting my arms around him that night – for that night he drove his car into his garage – closed the garage door with the car running – he died – what could I have said to change his destiny – or a dentist who I spoke to at length one evening – that night he shot himself – it goes on – what could I have said – to change the lives of so many - I didn't choose the path of right choices – so my memory challenges my present – since 1987 to present – the correction was made – I believe so fervently – once the truth is achieved – application is the only remaining factor to be implemented – I believe in the totality of selflessness – the self-centered person I was – restricted me in every area of my life – prevented me from being the person I am today – what am I today – I just want to give for the purity of giving – I want to have compassion for my fellow beings – these are truths inside of me – I must apply – I must implement – in the cacophony of our world society at present – principles are lost – it is hard for me to believe that in the year 2008 – war is a reality – killing one another is a reality – the horror of a mother - father – or wife – losing their son or daughter – or husband – the loved ones coming back without an arm or leg – I feel with great intensity my surroundings – I must always stay focused – never digress – my only purpose is to be of use to mankind – keeping the Four Absolutes in the foreground of my life – this may seem a bit off - from my story of life – it is not - this is happening now - with me – I have caught up with me - in life – so all these reflections – past memories – feelings going through my soul – are realities – the summations of a lifetime – I do not live in the past – I profit by the past – I live the present – I think about the future – a simple format – I wonder sometimes if there should be a class in our school system – college level – or any level – where teachings of understanding – are present – where compassion – tolerance – thinking of one another – is the code – where giving instead of taking is the arrangement – I can only imagine what our world would reap – if this philosophy were in place - in the forming years - of the children of today – it took me fifty-four years to truly put someone's welfare ahead of my own – it took me fifty-four to stop singing that song – doe - ray – me- me – me – self is most insidious - it can justify – it can rationalize – it can move a mountain – with self apparition – the time is drawing near for me to end this story – a month ago I lost another animal – Abigail – she died of cancer – she was so beautiful – so loving – the emptiness that encompasses me - pounds at my inner – it just never stops - the tears come – ever so often – they just flow – I am that little boy again – being dropped off at that orphanage – the feelings of loneliness will never dissipate – I am saddled with the solitude of these feelings for the rest of my living days – I have three German Shepherds left – Lady Jane – Hansie – Ricky – they are all the same age – I cannot fathom the loss of these three – there is such a paradox running through me – I have the total direction and power of the Master - within me – I have loneliness – beyond comprehension - within me - I have followed His direction – it has taken me over four years to write this story – not every day of course - the words that are down - on the pages that were read – is my story – the flow has been continuous – may you stand tall among the giants of humanity – and when you reach your destination – as I have reached mine – may you find what I have found – that the end was but a beginning – I will forever remain teachable – it is that teacha-bility - that makes me a true servant – after all is said – after all is done – I am but a servant of the Master -

APPENDICES

Selected writings 1988-2007

1988

It is an honor – and a privilege - to be used as an instrument – to be of service to humanity –

1988

One does not have to be educated – to love -

1988

Dignity is not owned by the rich – nor thrown away by the poor – it resides in the souls of mankind to endure the ages – hunger has no dignity – yet it survives – it flourishes in the streets of our major cities – where the downtrodden struggle to stay alive – Skid Row is the last stop for many – a section of life haunted by despair and heart-break – yet it exists – let us join to minimize – or wipe out hunger in these areas – and to restore dignity – if only for a brief moment – to the many unwanted denizens of our society –

1989

Skid Row is the last stop in our society – there is no middle class – there are no poor - there are no rich – the residents only – the broken – the disillusioned souls – still to come alive – my sister – my brother – my loves – I feel clean – when I walk among the multitudes –

1989

More credence is spent on ideas than on action – ideas do not put out a fire – the fire burns deep into the soul of mankind – the fire of greed – the fire of selfishness – the fire of self seeking – the burning fire of impurities - dishonesty – covered by the askance and most oblique justifications of wrong doings the world of worlds will ever know – love – the progression of time has put man on the moon – space walks – traveling at 17,000 mph – these were once ideas – I know – but until implemented – stayed dormant – everything is moving so fast – eyes cannot focus – minds wander – emotions stray – principles lie in wait – truths are flung – giving way to seeds of degradation – how simple it would be – to start all over again – to care – to have compassion - tolerance – to be free of the shackles of wants – to give freely – to think of someone else –

1990
Compassion – understanding – and tolerance – must surface – if mankind is to survive –

1991
Love and caring – are but dormant words – triggered only by constructive action –

1991
People always want to change people – educate people – make distinctions by color – sex - etc. – our world has segregated the segregated –

1991
Hunger is a terrible fiber – in the realities of life – Skid Rows are realities in every major city in our country – this is where hunger wedges it's empty vial into the souls of an already saddened – and despaired – society of life –

1993
May you stand tall among the giants of humanity – and when you reach your destination as I have reached mine – may you find what I have found – that the end was but a beginning –

1994
I am not out to change anyone – only to comfort the soul – to still the racing mind for a moment – to give back to humanity the courage it has given me to carry on – to be an example of caring – to stand tall among the multitudes – not ahead – nor behind – to see my brother – to see my sister – with purity – honesty – unselfishness and love – to segregate not the child from the adult – the black from the white – the men from the women – the gay from the straight – the Christian from the non – the rich from the poor - the sick from the

well – our society has segregated the segregated – beyond any human comprehension – permitting the vial of corruption – deceit – hate – greed – to permeate the area of love designated by the Maker – encapsulated for the future of mankind to visit – allow the human to lay their head – where it will glean the most solace –

1995

The world has changed – fear is prevailing in our society – seeds of doubt in our justice system – overpopulation pounding our cities with decaying values – selfishness spilling over the pot of greed – surfacing to un proportional degrees – yet – I have seen through my own experience – the communion of people – the caring – the love – the dedication – tireless volunteers working to serve humanity – where everyone is equal – color has no value – and religion is in God's hands –

1995 – The marriage

Today is the beginning of your lives as a unit – you are both in God's grace as you step out from this day – as husband and wife – existing in your frame work will be a communion of love – understanding – tolerance – uncompromised purity of thought – towering honesty – unselfishness to the degree that there is only one thought between you – that is – of each other – for each other – these are the prevailing principles – that exist at this moment – and for a lifetime – it is an honor for me to preside on this day that will consume your memory – for time to come – allow your joys to be shared – your triumphs – your dreams – your hopes – hide nothing from each other – for there is no room for darkness in purity – love flows abundantly when the water is clear – there are times in life when sadness prevails – hold each other – cry with each other – feel the agony today – so that the sun may shine somewhat tomorrow – be a beacon of hope for the human race – let your lives be an example for those to follow – and let your love for each other spill over – for the betterment of humanity –

1995

If I had ever been told in 1987 that I was going to be approaching half million meals served to the society known as Skid Row downtown Los Angeles – that eight struggling years were to pass – I might have let the boat go by – to each and everyone of the thousands of people that have contributed to Frontline in any form – it is an honor to thank you – to be alive to say thank you – you the people are a tribute to mankind – you have restored dignity for a brief moment to – the unwanted – despaired of our society – for that moment – the communion of humanity is complete –

1995

No one ever wins in a tragedy – yet they occur every day throughout our world – no city - or town - nor village - ever escapes the holocaust of tragedy – it is what it is – the darkest of the dark – the sorrow beyond compromise – the imagery never ends – the devastation of the soul – the wound without healing – there is no place on earth one can go to escape – this never ending light of darkness

1995

I have fought long and hard - for the essence of God's will - for these past eight years – to be an instrument – to serve humanity – to receive nothing for what I do – to weep sometimes in the solitude of my own soul – to marvel at the wonderment of 465,000 meals served to the unwanted – to look at the shuttered eyes of our mainstream populace – to see first hand the money that is procured at the expense of the fallen – we are a people stagnated in a whirlpool of our own society – trying desperately to find a little peace of mind –

1996

What better gift for me to give my fellow beings but a smile – a look of love into the eyes of the despaired – to have acceptance of what a human being is – rather than to try to change the soul – to be an example of purity – honesty – unselfishness – and love – to have no motives – to be free of all ideology – to focus only on the betterment of mankind -

1996

When the Editor of Frontline Today asked me to write something about reaching 500,000 meals served – I procrastinated a few
weeks – trying to find prolific words with profound and deep meaning –much to my dismay I could not come up with anything – I have
not the ability to put into words the magnitude - nor the overwhelming feeling I have in my heart – most of us have seen the Rose Bowl
filled to capacity on New Year's Day – take one moment – visualize
it – multiply it by five – five hundred thousand meals – these meals
were served in an area known as Skid Row – downtown Los Angeles
– on the streets – not protected by buildings or fences – the learning
process was not easy – yet – the learning took place – looking back
over the years since 1987 – I see thousands of faces – I see the hands
that reach for our meals – I see those dark streets at night with the
fires – I see the hopeless – the helpless – I see the strong – the weak
– I see the wounds on the body – I see the sickness – I see the agony
– I see the dead – I have seen mankind - bleed – I have seen mankind
- cry out for help – I have seen the despair of the human soul – I have
touched – held – rocked many people that will never see the dawn of
a new day – the learning process did take place – the ability for me
to feel with such passion – to hear the cries with such clarity – to
sense my fellow man with a purity that runs so deep – to see the
cleanliness of the ragged clothed being – to know the true meaning
of purity – to comprehend honesty to its fullest – to enter the world
of unselfishness – free of any wants – to know love – I thank God for
allowing me to be His instrument – I thank my wife who stood by my
side – I thank all the people who gave to this powerful display of
God's will –

1997

.....In February - Frontline and Ray suffered a great loss – the
tragic and very untimely death of one of our beautiful volunteers -
Josh Randell – the following is an obituary written by Ray about this
young man – a "Humanitarian in Training"- as Ray would call him –
......Frontline will be forever indebted for your service to
mankind – for your love – for dignified caring for the people of Skid

Row – downtown Los Angeles – for your purity of thought – your uncomplicated measure of unselfishness – the enduring hours you have put in at the kitchen for the sole purpose of giving – with no return – so as not to compromise your values – when I told you to peel each egg with love – you looked at me inquisitively – I explained it one more time – a smile came to your face and the connection was made – at age fifteen you have touched so many – you have shadowed - the hopeless - the despaired – the tired – the weak – the strong – with your entity of compassion – you have crossed the final pathway that will endure eternity – as each of us take our step – your hand will guide us to meet the Master –

1998

The world has changed – fear is prevailing in our society – seeds of doubt in our justice system – overpopulation pounding our cities with decaying values – selfishness spilling over the pot of greed – surfacing to un proportional degrees –

I wrote this preceding paragraph several years ago – much to my dismay the picture has not changed – as I have grown older and the importance of self has diminished – I feel with great intensity the feelings – both joyous and tragic – of humanity's swirling existence – when that girl drove those two children into the lake a few years ago – the picture I will never forget is when the diver found the car – and how the babies' hands were clutching the window – I relive that moment when the car was submerging – those two children wondering for a brief moment where their mother was – and what was going on – before fear and epic tragedy set in – oh my God – I feel the horror – I feel their pain – I feel their fear – the only solace in my heart is knowing they are sitting with God – warmed by His thoughts – it does not only hold true for this side of the spectrum – experiencing the joy of giving and

seeing the face light up of another – the triumphs – the successes of others - to be able to sense the love generated within a wolf pack for each other – to sense the lose of a bear cub when the mother is shot – a fallen deer brought down by the hunter in the wilds – her fawn looking on - there are all sorts of feelings that I feel when freedom of self prevails – loneliness beyond reproach – understanding of others – the agony and ecstasy of life itself –the freer of self I've become – the obstacles are in the way between myself and the truth –truth and principles have become one – justifications obsolete – rationalizations extinct – the wonderment of seeing a sunset on the ocean is a reality uncluttered by the cacophony of our society – there are tears in my heart for the human race – there is pain in my frame for humanity – mankind teeters on the brink of self-destruction – the animals are being crowded out of their habitat – when all the wildlife ceases to be …are we next?

1998

One of the greatest – no – the greatest treasure of life – I believe – is freedom of self – to stand amid the center of a hurricane – and have calm of soul – the awareness I sense – to know – to feel – tranquility within my heart – not to be ruffled or swayed in any direction – nor to be steeped in fear –worry or discontentment – the eye of the storm centered in my being – relinquishing only love – compassion – understanding – for the human race – to be able to put the welfare of others ahead of my own – to be able to feel someone else's pain – to share in their dream – to avoid argument – to avoid retaliation – to respect the viewpoints of others – to be able to listen – there were years I was involved with self – the lack of freedom – disallowing the comfort of giving freely – the fears that are attached to the constant thought of myself – echoed consistently through my very existence – this is why I believe – freedom of self – is the greatest gift I received in this world of ours – I believe this is why I love the streets of Skid Row so much – I feel the intensity of humanity – it is an honor for me to serve the people of the streets – a privilege to be used as an instrument – eleven years will be coming up soon – I am as excited now as I was December 5, 1987 – to pull my truck up at 5th and Crocker – downtown Los Angeles – I am as humbled now as I was when I left downtown the first time – I take no credit for the demonstration - of this powerful miracle – for the betterment of mankind – it was orchestrated by the Master – truly the Touch Of The Master's Hand – not only did He involve me –but thousands of others contributing to

His pure entity of love – for his children of the streets – but are not we His children also - a circle of compassion – a ring of hope – a smile for many – a tear for some – thank you again dear people for being involved on this journey – for without you – the journey would be but a dream – devoid of action-

1998

Frontline will surpass 600,000 meals to the residents of Skid Row – downtown Los Angeles – what was only to be a few meals served has gone into another dimension – a dimension where love – compassion – understanding – superseded the obvious of serving food – it was dictated to me in 1987 not to solicit any money – nor receive any compensation for what I was to embark on – thinking it was only going to be a few days out of my life – I was obedient to the calling – had I known it was going to consume eleven years of my life and still going – it might have a different story – yes – it would have been a different story – a miracle has taken place – an unexplained happening – a phenomenon if I may – the principles by which Frontline is guided purity – honesty – unselfishness and love prevail – at times – most arduous – with so many people to answer to – I want to thank each and every person for helping me to fulfill the calling I had in 1987 – for it was not only my calling – but each person that has given – with their love – their support for the betterment of our society – Frontline has 650 people - that support in a financial way on a regular basis – such a small populous – such a mammoth job – Frontline running since 1987 – the food given out – inestimable – the thousands of people that are involved – the children in the schools – the churches – the synagogues – please stand tall my dear friends – you have all been a part of a true miracle – I am not out to reach one of you that has given – but all of you that have given – if I had the ability to touch the heart of each – I would – allow my spirit – my love for humanity – my cries of despair – my agonies – my joys – my tears – my smile - my triumphs - my losses – allow them to be with you – please allow me to walk with each of you for the rest of your life – as you have walked with me during my life –

1999

I have been serving food to the people of Skid Row going on twelve years – this is what it seems like to the naked eye – the depth by which I see human nature far exceeds any school room rhetoric – Skid Row Los Angeles is not an easy life for any human being down on their luck – the perception of so many – is that these are people – who are lazy – people who don't want to work – people who want to sponge off society – or people who just want to use drugs – drink alcohol – prostitute their values – if anyone does believe these things – please be my guest and come with me on a two day venture - make an effort to survive two nights on the streets – I want to thank every participant of Frontline down through the years – every person that has put in so much thought – I thank the thousands of people that have supported Frontline – not one of the people that so much as touched Frontline – had a malice thought toward these people of Skid Row – a miracle – this is what made it work – I have touched in the literal sense tens of thousands – looked in the eyes of so many broken souls – rocked and held so many more – I have melded with the sweat – from their sun drenched bodies in the summer – I have felt the chill of their form – from the rain and cold – I have visited the prisons when they were in – I have waited for them to come out – went to the hospital when they were under John or Jane Doe – I have seen the harassment of a group of people beyond the limits of human degradation – the last two years on Skid Row – I have seen the attempt to cleanout the whole area of humans – that inhabit the streets – talk about Albania – we have it in our city – I wonder who is responsible? –I went downtown with 1,500 meals last summer – made a few stops – the last one was on San Julian across the street from the new mission – as I was serving – three rent a-cops and their boss came over to me and told me to move – that they didn't want this element in front of their mission - "this element"- can you imagine "this element" is black – the people of the streets made a circle around myself – the man and the rent a-cops – I certainly did not want any trouble – I told them so – but I was appalled and sickened by the episode – there are many more people getting arrested on Skid Row than any other part of the city – like this is where all the money is – if this kind of street sweeping and degrading of mankind were the order of the day – let's say – in Redondo Beach or Beverly Hills – how long would it last - are we not all God's children - or does He segregate His flock - I want to give water to the thirsty – soup to the one who is cold – I truly want to comfort the soul – I want to look deep into the eyes of my brother and sister – I want to be my brother's keeper – I want to mingle among the multitudes – I want to feel their heartbeats – I want to share their tears – I want the people of the streets - to feel – my presence – as I feel theirs – the mutual respect of them for me – me for them – is the bond – the link - that cements the principle of everlasting faith between two entities – depriving not the force of love – it was dictated to me some twelve years ago – a calling if you will – by a higher being – to receive no compensation nor solicit any money for what I was to embark on – to serve humanity in the area known as Skid Row – downtown Los Angeles – I have fulfilled the dictates to the best of my belief – 630,000 meals have been served – thousands of people connected with Frontline – giving for the purity of giving – a true miracle for each of us – I thank God for allowing me to be an instrument of His will – I thank the people of Frontline for their unselfish act of support – I have survived with you – and you with me – together a difference has been made –

1999
My first trip to Skid Row – I met a man of 43 years of age – his name - Leo – he was from Cuba – hung on the corner of 5th and San Pedro with a Cuban contingency of about 12-14 people – we greeted each other – from that day forth – which exceeds twelve years – we remained friends – last month – on Tuesday November 24th – we spent the morning – he hugged and kissed me – I gave him $3 – but more than that – a reflection on eleven years – for the next day he died – I did not find out until the next week – December 5th – which marked - the 11th year - to the day - I met him – I saw him through all of his times during this period – he was stabbed in the back very seriously – he was run over by a passing car – most serious – he survived on the most tormented streets our city of Los Angeles put forth – he is a soul for the ages – he worked the first seven years on the streets

with Frontline – where we survived a multitude of confrontations – when 1500 people would line up on a Saturday morning – where 500 on a Tuesday for chili dogs – he befriended all of the Frontline regulars at that time – he was a true part of the beginning of Frontline – we cried together – we laughed – he called me Papa in his broken English – what saddens me most – more than anything else – is that they found his body some 3 or 4 days later in his room – which means he died alone – in that 5x5 room on Skid Row – with no one by his side – no one to comfort him – so my heart is most heavy – not because he died – I know he is with God – most likely asking for three dollars – but because he was alone in a room on Skid Row – Los Angeles – I pray he died in peace – I pray he died without fear – he was truly one of God's servants – for the past twelve years – I have been on these streets of Skid Row – I have received no compensation nor solicited any money – I was directed to serve food to the unwanted of our society – I have done so – over 617,000 – God given – God inspired – a long - arduous road – I have seen death on the streets – never spoken about it – the body put in a bag - shipped out – I have seen a gal with cerebral palsy - get her throat cut – put in a dumpster – no authority following up on it – I have seen the people of Skid Row pushed from one side of the street to the other – when days are hot – no water – when it's cold – no soup – I have seen prejudice beyond anything - elsewhere in our society today – I deal with the poorest of the poor – I have become a people of the streets – I see no women or man – no children or adults – I see no color or group – I see only God's children – equality among humans is our only salvation – I deal with four principles – purity – honesty - unselfishness and love – these principles have carried me through the past twelve years – fighting the bureaucracy of Los Angeles – I could serve all of Skid Row with a little help – but because there is no money to be made from my organization – people are afraid of it - I only want to hold the head of my fallen brother or sister - I only want to console - the mind - body - of the unwanted – I want to feel their pain – the people of Skid Row ask for so little – allow me to be an instrument - to fulfill a moment – in their lives – to give them a moment of peace – not to change anyone – not to give them a new philosophy of life –

but to love each – for what each stands for – to accept the beauty of the downtrodden – the people of Skid Row have taught me so much about life – a lesson could be learned – but nobody is listening – dear Leo – you gave me love with no conditions – you gave me hope with your smile – you gave me courage with your being – you gave me strength through your eyes – God will take care of you for eternity – you will never be alone again –

1999
If one person lives long enough to look back and see his or her life - and is able to reflect for a moment – a library will be filled with memories – the joys – the tears – the sorrows – the direction I should have taken and didn't – the ones I took and shouldn't have – the goals set that were achieved – the goals that have laid by the wayside and never achieved – a career that stumbled and yet great moments to be remembered – the death of loved ones – the time I was never able to say good-bye to my mother – for her husband at the time – took her up in an airplane – she was not to be moved – because of a stroke - she had a bad heart – she died over Baltimore in that plane due to heart failure – he died – he paid a terrific price 14 months later – cancer had reduced him to nothing – he was never able to spend my mother's money – the love I had for my Grandfather and godfather – I loved these two men with all my heart to this day – the loneliness I felt in that orphanage early in my childhood – for two and a half years – the tears I shed – the memory is so vivid – I can see every corner every hall – every room –I can smell the bathroom – I can see the dormitory with sixty or so seventy beds – when we were on our way to sleep – there was not one sound from any of us – for if we spoke – we would be strapped by a women named Mary – I still remember – we were all trying to survive – we never snitched on anyone or anything – we were loyal to one another – we never showed our weakness to the people whose care we were in – for if we did we would pay for it dearly – I remember one time they forced liver down my throat – it made me so sick – I was suppose to eat anything they put in front of me – I didn't – they made an example of me – each time – how I remember – when one of the older boys ran away and get

caught – they would put us in a big hall – sit us down – put the boy on a long table – hold him down and beat him – then turn to us and say – "if anyone tries to run away – this is what is going to happen to you" – how well I remember that – I was a bed-wetter – again they made an example of me – telling of my bed-wetting to the throng of boys – none of the boys made fun of me or ever spoke of it – they knew what was going on – but I remember – once in a great while my Aunt would come and visit me – for she lived in New York very close to the orphanage – I would be so happy when I saw her – I begged her to take me with her – when she left I cried – cried – and cried some more for days – I would have a lonely feeling inside of me – I remember when they put me in another home in Troy New York – I ran away to my Grandfather's in Albany – seventeen miles away – I planned my own escape from that one – a story in itself –I was seven at the time – I ran to my Grandfather who lived in a cellar under a nursing home my Grandmother ran – down the stairs I went – the door was locked – I cried and hit the door saying "Grandpa – Grandpa please let me in"- the lock turned and he opened the door – there he stood 6' 2" looking down at me – I cried to him saying "please don't let them take me back – please Grandpa – please"- he picked me up in his arms and said – "nobody is going to take you away anymore"- little did I know – that moment I spent with him – those words - in broken English that he said – would forever be instilled in my very soul – that was around 1940 – the moment is as fresh today 1999 as then – how lucky I am – I stayed with him in the cellar – a small bed by his side – for the next three and a half years we listened to all the radio shows of the time – Jack Benny – The Great Gildersleeve - Amos and Andy – Duffy's Tavern - etc – how beautiful – how warm my heart is – even today – thinking about that period of my life – Grandfather all week – my Godfather on Sunday – my Godfather died when I was eleven – what a lose – he was a member of the Black Hand – I was surrounded by these beautiful people every Sunday – I was protected on the streets in the neighborhood from any harm – the beauty parlor was the front for gambling and the numbers racket and whatever else I didn't see – I was loved so very much by all the constituents the Black Hand preceded the Mafia – when my Godfather died I cried again – that lonely feeling – one more time – maybe it had never left – three and a half years later my Grandfather died – I was fifteen – my heart was empty – I cried one more time – out of loneliness – that feeling inside of me – that hurt – that sorrow has never left me – I can still feel my Grandfather's arms around me when he picked me up when I was seven – and my Godfather's hand touching the top of my head with love ever so gently – at this same time around eleven years of age – I will have a moment in my life that will be forever frozen in my memory – my natural Father's name was Raymond Jay Johnston – also my name at the time – I had only seen him three times in my life before this moment – this was the fourth – a railroad station in Albany, New York was the place – my Aunt got me ready – I asked her – what should I call him – she said call him Dad – he's your father – I met him in that station – we sat alone – we talked – he held my hand – I could feel his energy – I could feel the compassion and love he had for me – when I looked into his eyes – tears came – I could sense the loneliness he felt – to this day I don't remember a word we said – if any – only feelings – maybe we never said anything – he gave me two dollars – put his arms around me for a moment – walked through the big doors to the train yard – I stood alone and watched him leave – this would be the last time I would ever see him – as I reflected back – years later – the loneliness he must have felt as that train moved away from Albany – I have a sense of him looking out a window – knowing in his heart that he would never see me again – that must have been one of the loneliest train rides – I only wish I could have shared it with him – twenty or so years later on February eighteenth – which is my birthday – a great sense of my father Raymond Johnston came over me – he was the topic of conversation for some reason with me – around the end of March 1965 – I received a letter from back East from my father's brother – the letter went something like this –"on February eigh-teenth – your father got up from his bed and went over to the dresser drawer – picked up these pictures (baby pictures) and said 'this is my son's birthday'- he was so weak he could not hold a glass of water in his hand – he died twelve days later"- at that moment I cried one more time – for I knew my father's loneliness – the pictures were old and used – how many times did he touch them – I was told many years prior he was dead – finding out now was a different story – that lonely feeling came over me once more – I was that little boy in that orphanage again – but at that moment I knew I had a father who loved me very dearly – the next twenty-one years would be filled glory and agony – I never learned to read too good or spell – was not good in my school work – but was blessed with a good body – so I excelled in sports – but by eighteen – drinking was a big part of my life – also – life was in front of me – the night life I loved and so I lived – three years in the Marine Corps – started an acting career – four children – a fifth died at birth – a sorrowful moment – a few months prior – my wife at the time pounded her pregnant stomach – with hate and distain for me – for by this time alcohol had taken its toll on me – I was old before my time – bleeding internally – sores on my body – unshaven – very gaunt – audio hallucinations – I no longer could do any work of any kind – I was inarticulate – I was dying – In July 1969 I held a bottle of gin in my hand and uttered these words – "please God help me – I don't want to drink this"- July 1999 will be thirty years - my cry of despair that day in July 1969 was heard – my career resumed very slowly – I learned how to talk again – by then my talent had diminished to nothing – I went back to acting classes for two years – '78-79' by 1980 I was back in full swing - I was to do a Broadway play – it hung for a year – by 1982 it was over – the money could not be raised – I had a moment in 1981 where I did a play – a director by the name of Danny Mann saw it – he directed - The Rose Tattoo – Butterfield 8 – I Want To Live – all Academy Award winners – and the stage play Come Back Little Sheba – on Broadway – which won a Tony – he wanted me for his play – so I did make it – even though nobody knows it – the play never got off the ground – broken dreams one more time – By 1986 I was most despondent – I no longer wanted to act – I had done hundreds of shows – always playing the bad guy – I cut all ties in Los Angeles – took off in my truck to places unknown – pounding my dashboard – crying out to God to show me the way – any way – that He wanted me to go – another cry of despair – and so it was – I was to return to Los Angeles – much against my will - I did so – it was revealed to me – not through voices – but definitely through a Power – to receive no money nor solicit any money – I was to serve food to the residents of Skid Row downtown Los Angeles – I had no problem in being obedient to His will – on December 5, 1987 on a rainy morning – 111 peanut butter and jelly sandwiches were served – July 1999 – over 635,000 meals have been served – a true miracle – for twelve years I have been on the streets of Skid Row – downtown Los Angeles – I have been with the people – the downtrodden of our society – the forgotten souls of mankind – I have fought the elements – the bureaucracy of our city – I have seen harassment – I have seen death – murder – rape - I worked through my own sickness (heart problems) – no help in sight – I know the story of life – the greatest gift I have is freedom of self – from these streets of Los Angeles – to the Rose Garden in Washington DC – to meet the President of the United States – I took all of the memories of each person I touched with me on that memorable day – it was their triumph – when I came back to the streets the people knew they were alongside of me in Washington – the wisdom of God – the power of His will has been displayed – thousands of people have been warmed by His presence – a true miracle –my story ends here – I was obedient to His calling – equality among the human race – compassion for all – understanding beyond – honesty through the eyes of the beholder – freedom of self within the heart of each other - purity of mind – purity of body – purity of soul – the inner existence of the making of mankind – there can be no love seeding - when distrust and deceit are paramount factors in the make up of the human race – it is His miracle – I am only the story teller – the instrument used – at times most reluctantly – I have learned much – since I was that four year old in that New York orphanage – crying in a corner out of loneliness – I still have the feelings of loneliness in my heart – I am still that little boy crying in that orphanage – when I make that final trip and meet the Master Himself – I know then and only then – that my tears and loneliness will be only memories of warmth and joy –

2000
Principles don't lie –

2000
To be of service to the Master – this is the only reason for my existence – the disobedience of His order – will result only in disharmony – where selfishness – deceit – impurities of mind – body - soul – stand forever maligning His will –

2000 – Good Night Danny –
The horror of what happened to you dear friend – will last what lifetime I have left – you have given me the best tribute a person can give another – that is you wanted the principles of which I live by – to prevail in your being – for the better part of fifteen years you listened – executed these principles with a passion – you became a man among men – you lived your life – found your way to peace of mind – and a God that guided you – on December 17thof 1999 you and I talked on the phone from California to Tennessee as we did many times these past four years – we spoke of how happy you were – how you found a lady friend that you cared about – we talked about God – how when I met Him – I would let Him know a thing or two – that I would make sure He took care of you – we talked this way for years – for I was seventeen years older than you – we laughed so much – we cried at times – the spirit of understanding grew – you called me many times to see if all was well – how I remember the moments of revelations – when you got the point I was trying to make –well dear Danny – you have surpassed me in all areas – you dear friend have become the teacher – I am the student – you dear friend are with the Master –all knowing – transcending His knowledge to you - you have a most beautiful light that encompasses your soul – a smile on your face – that will last forever – you dear Danny were born January 10th 1951 – on January 19th 2000 while you were asleep on the couch – fate came – even though I was 3000 miles away – I can feel the bullets enter your body – I have woken up many night since – I cry for you dear friend - for I am only a mortal – my only wish is that it were me – good night dear Danny – we will meet soon - walk the path with God - as eternity embraces our souls –

2000 – Fundraiser

My hope is to bring people together from all walks of life – with one sole purpose – that is to enhance the betterment of mankind – to bring in the new millennium with understanding – compassion – with tolerance – honesty - integrity – to propagate selflessness – to encourage equality among our fellow beings – this is my hope – Martin Luther King had a dream – let this be a reality for the new millennium – the salvation of the human race – rests - on these principles – Frontline has served over 635,000 meals to the unwanted and disparaged souls of our society in an area known as Skid Row in downtown Los Angeles since1987 – this event is solely dedicated to elevate the awareness that Frontline is not about the serving of food – but rather about our concern for humanity – the food is but a vehicle – that transmits – compassion for the heart – love of the soul – purity of thought – withstanding honesty – unselfishness – to guide ourselves through the maze of our turbulent society -

2000

I have stated on many different occasions the freer I became of self – the more acutely I felt the surroundings of life – the beat of the soul – the joy of another's triumph – the agony of a tear from a lost being – to be of service to the Master – this is the only reason for my existence – the disobedience of His order – will result only in disharmony – where selfishness – deceit – impurities of mind – body – soul – stand forever maligning His will - I wrote this passage not so long ago – what a paradise humanity would exist in – if this were the rule of the day – I cried as a little boy out of loneliness – nothing stood between my loneliness and life – so the tears were always streaming down my face – here I am one more time – many years later – loneliness fills my heart – tears are shed – nothing stands between my Priscilla and myself – the smell of her coat – the touch of her coat – the strength of her body – the ears back as she speeds to my arms – the keen eyes – the protective nature – the way she speaks – to let me know what she wants – the uncomplicated – simple devotions she radiates from her persona – she never lies – she never cheats – she is never dishonest – she never has impure thoughts – she just loves –

Priscilla is my dog – my mind knows this – but the lonely feeling inside my heart does not – it just hurts – there are no rationalizations or justifications – that can take away the sorrow – nor can I compromise the feelings – they just are – this is what I bring to the people of Skid Row – a human being - stripped of self – so that the language of the heart – is ever so prevalent – and the power of the Master ever so present –

2000

I am sitting outside my house this October day – year 2000 – it is warm – with a slight breeze warming its way around my never-ending sight of imagination – I am with two of my dogs – one Priscilla – the other Lady – my girl Priscilla is most sick with cancer – which promoted me to write a little bit – I visualized a rock of great proportions – one hundred miles up – deep – across – I visualized a hummingbird coming once every two thousand years to sharpen its beak – I visualized a cube of granite worn down to nothing – when the dust blew in a funnel sweep – one day of eternity had elapsed – I am on this earth but a short time – eternity is waiting for me – the joy of eternity – each moment filled with the wonderment of tranquility – the enlightenment of knowing all – the presence of God warming my soul – never again to feel pain – the essence of purity – to be in harmony with the Master – where honesty – unselfishness – and love play no factor – where the communion of my Grandfather – my Godfather – and the lonely father I never knew – will be so ever present – my dog Ben – my dog Priscilla – Samantha – Sonny – Hansie – Buster – Lady – and of course Little Ricky –will be sitting in line with that warm breeze of everlasting compassion and tolerance for the human race –for they too will be all knowing in the presence of the Father – the imagination travels far – yes indeed – but the destination is ever so bright – while I am alive – allow me to be an instrument of His will – to fulfill my destiny by helping humanity – to invoke the principles of purity – honesty and unselfishness – so that love will not be tarnished – I am still sitting outside – it is still October of the same day – year 2000 – thank you for hearing my heart –

2004

What became meaningful after thirty four and one half years? what became all knowing after thirty four and one half years of sobriety? why has it been so easy for me to understand the concept of Alcoholics Anonymous in its present form? here - after thirty four years plus is only one example why – the true realization of what I was dealing with came to me many years ago – maybe thirty three years ago when I was so very young on the program – I knew – truly what I was dealing with – that being alcohol – no more no less – remembering always that one fact – for that simple fact will carry me many years into the future – the ups the downs of life – the roads that go nowhere – the hills that must be climbed – the valleys that hurt with despair – the torments - the frustration – the disappointments - the joys – the faces that I will see and see no more – the summers – the falls – the winters - the springs – I must weather the storms of life – good or bad – I must live life as life unfolds – not swayed by fiction or fantasy – I must put forth an effort always - to do the Will of God – to care for His flock – I have and always will remember what I am dealing with – alcohol – though living life these past thirty four years - the cunningness of alcohol has been defined in my soul so many times – by the downfall of people who did not know what they were dealing with – the one word - cunning - describes so well John Barleycorn – to enhance and define even further what I am dealing with let me use the word - baffling – again I turn to the thousands of people – the empty faces that ponder and are still pondering the eluding fact of what to deal with – cannot see in any way or form - the direction of hope – it will remain baffling to the end for most – I would like to inject the word - powerful – with my face down – a most gaunt – cadaverous looking human – sores on my body that would not heal – bleeding from the inside – audio and visual hallucinations – unable to grasp an idea of any kind – the inability to put words together – to make a simple sentence – to wander in a maze of confusion – to be riddled with fear - paranoia – to only be focused on one thing – alcohol – there was no life – no hope – only death – I welcomed death – a warm beautiful feeling – knowing the end was close – for now it only took one ounce of drink to render me immobile –

the power of alcohol – instant recall of how it was - remains ever so constant in the crevasses of my soul – my instincts knew that without help it would be too much for me – where was the answer to come from? – I could no longer think – my mind was shattered – the paralysis of my mouth made me mumble – and then it came – there is one who has all power – it filled my empty vat of hopelessness with my cry of despair - my words - July of 1969 were – "please God help me I don't want to drink this" – as I held a bottle of gin in my hand – unparallel fear of drink gripped me – for even though I wanted to drink – I could not – unknown to me at that time I found the power of God – a very small fragment of power - none the less - enough to carry me through the horror of sobering up – the d – tees - delirium tremors as it's called – the vile smell of alcohol seeping through my pores – the lights flashing through my head to my eyes – the trembling body pulsating in all directions – the physical pain griping parts of my body at different times – I was totally alone when all this was going on – again instant recall – the calm that came over me - days later - when it was all over – the warm breeze of August - I still remember – nothing was left – no trace of life as it was – my mind vacated of any thoughts whatsoever – if I was to step into the picture of half measures – it would be to no avail – I knew this from the nothingness of my being – the left over soul of a man at thirty six years of age – my cry of despair was answered – for I was to live – I truly stood at the turning point of life – the only cry from me was to ask for His protection and care with complete abandon –

My Cry of Despair –

Newsletter – November 2004 – Page 1

I see so many pictures of the streets of Skid Row in down town Los Angeles – I see so many faces – I see so many hands reaching – I hear so many cries of despair – I feel the hopelessness of so many – I sense the fear of many that will never see the next day – I sense the fear in many that live on the streets daily – come December 5th 2004 it will be 17 years I have spent on the streets of Skid Row – what started with 111 peanut butter and jelly sandwiches on a cold and rainy day that December 5th 1987 – has now turned into over 792,000 meals served on these same streets – verboten streets to say the least – what looks like food – tastes like food – even smells like food – is not what I serve – I serve purity of mind - body and soul to the denizens of Skid Row – there have been thousands that I have come in contact with – so aware are the people of the streets – they can sense fraud – they can sense a con – they trust no one – people that come to Skid Row are out to change them – rehabilitate them – give them a sermon – show them there is a better way to go – when I look my brother or sister in the eye – I only see God's child – I see a forgotten soul of the human race – I am only to touch them - and them to me – the purity of my soul must touch the purity of their soul – the dishonesty of our society is most prevalent - it trickles to the bottom and must be stamped out with honesty – so when I say - I care – it must be backed up with action – devoid of any self seeking motive – for if there is one splinter of oblique dishonesty – the acute awareness of the people of the streets will pick up on it – when I give of myself – I must give freely – I must give purely – I must give with no conditions – I must give with the totality of freedom of self – this - in order to attain the unselfishness of self – so I am interwoven with humanity in a section known as Skid Row in downtown Los Angeles – where my soul is touched by so many – where death lurks in that unknown corner of emptiness – where despair is the order of the day – the society of Skid Row is most unique – the moment they live in - is now – the tomorrows may never come for many – the walk across the street to a new life – is much too far for most – there is a beat - an undercurrent – a care for one another - and yet not – a sharing of what one has – giving to another – a stranger cannot see what goes on – they only see the dismay – the rubble of souls – they cannot see the watchful eye for one to another – the torn fragments of their bodies as they move through each day is a sight to behold – for they truly can survive – the code of ethics – the respect they have for each – coupled with the instant attack - sometimes a killing when disrespect comes into view – these are the streets of Skid Row where I have spent 17 years of my life – it is an honor for me to be of service to His flock – I take no credit – I just followed the directions – if I could somehow put into words the humility that comes forth in my being as a result of the thousands of people that supported this endeavor – I would be a poet – I am not a poet – so to each - my thank you - for being a part of this miracle – I give each of all - a piece of the fragments of Skid Row –

I wrote this piece in November of 2004 for the Frontline News letter – here it is 2005 same month – I read it for the first time – I rarely reread the pieces I wrote – I get emotional when I got through reading the article – I realized I could not add anything to what I already wrote – things have not changed – the street is the same – over 830,000 meals have been served – that is a change – several more deaths – more frailties – as the years go on – more influx of new people to take the place of the dead – but the purity of the brutality of Skid Row remains the same – the hunger to stay alive for some – the resolve of the end - for many – the vicious circle of torment that encompasses the souls that wander the night with the rats - that are so friendly – not wanting to see the day – the long days moving from one side of the street to the other – never being able to get comfortable – the police come by so often to enforce the order given to them – the J – walking tickets – the street sweeps that take every possession a man or women has – leaving them nothing – standing alone – to start all over again – to wind up with nothing – one more time – when it is hot - it is hard to find water – when they sit in the shade on these hot days – the police come by and have them move to the other side of the street where the sun shines - order of the day – when it is cold – I have seen both man and women – shivering – no shirt – no socks – no jacket – add a little rain – the misery becomes acute – the water dripping from their forehead – trying to curl up like a snail in a shell - to shun the chill - no end in site – the eyes of despair that inhabit the soul for so many – the arrogance displayed by some – the survival mode for others – yes there is whisky – gin - vodka for some – a Cisco for others – cocaine – heroin – uppers – downers – there are female prostitutes – male prostitutes – also just plain people that prostitute their very existence and ideals – there are liars – con artists – manipulators to the highest degree – there are thieves – there are dealers on the streets that will deal in anything – from toothpicks to drugs to humans - yes there are murderers – there are rapist – child molesters – along with doctors – lawyers – businessman – wife beaters – there are people that have so many different personalities - one does not know from one day to the next day which one - one is talking to – there is the wounded of the soul and spirit – there is the wounded of the body – open gashes that ooze infected liquid – swollen eyes and faces that tell the horror of the streets – there are no tomorrows for many – only the memory of how it use to be – the young child in his or her mothers arms – hunger of the core – hunger of the psyche – compassion – understanding – tolerance - this is what I serve to the individuals that inhabit the streets of Skid Row – I accept each – as each is – I do not in any way make an effort to change anyone – nor if I could - want to – I have been blessed – I realize this – I take no credit for the thousands I have been privileged to touch on the streets – nor the many hundreds of volunteers that work tirelessly day after day for the past eighteen years – to the scores upon scores - many times over – may I say - that without the monetary support given so freely – the miracle of this entity would lie dormant – "it is an honor for me to be of service to His flock – I take no credit – I just followed the directions – if I could somehow put into words the humility that comes forth in my being as a result of the thousands of people that supported this endeavor – I would be a poet – I am not a poet – so to each - my thank you - for being a part of this miracle – I give each of all - a piece of the fragments of Skid Row – "

2006
Come December 5th 2006 – nineteen years will have passed since I made my first trip down town to Skid Row – I served 111 peanut butter and jelly sandwiches that morning in about three minutes – a moment in my life time – never to be forgotten - come the end of this year 2006 – over 875,000 meals will have been served to the denizens of Skid Row – more important than the meals – is what really has been served – understanding – compassion – tolerance of mankind – a steady diet of giving for the purity of giving – this was

made possible by the dictates of the Master Himself – who put together this package – for some inexplicable reason – thousands of people - have put their touch to an entity - most powerful – have put their energy - to work – compiling a magnificent and most compelling force - for the betterment of the human race – thank you all - for the tears - that accompany the joys - of being a servant –

2007

The wonderment – the miracle - the power – the force – the giving – the honesty – the purity – the unselfishness – the love – are but words Frontline Foundation has nourished and implemented this philosophy from the beginning – given to Frontline by the Master Himself – to give for the purity of giving – to ask nothing in return – twenty years this December 5th 2007 will have passed – 111 peanut butter sandwiches were distributed with jelly – in about three minutes on that rainy morning – this December 5th over 908,000 meals will be surpassed – the thousands upon thousands of faces that I have seen – the thousands of hands that reached for the food – the thousands of volunteers that have emptied their silo – the old – the young – the deceased unfortunately – the five year olds are now twenty five - the high school students that came – are now married – and in the work force – so they come – some have been with Frontline the whole run – most over fifteen years – it was never about the food – it was about compassion – it was about tolerance – it was about caring – it was about the camaraderie of the whole entity – it was about understanding – a force for the betterment of mankind – to think of others – to for go self – to all – there are so many – my humble – most gracious – thank you -

Commencement Address at the Albany Academy

June, 1997

This is a moment - to be remembered - this is a moment that will be remembered - in the hearts - minds - bodies - and souls - of each and every one of you sitting here - this day - June 11, 1997 - The 184th Commencement - of the Albany Academy -

I congratulate each of you - that is graduating today - I want to thank - each one of you - for this beautiful - and prestigious - honor - you have bestowed upon me - it is both humbling - and heartwarming - I welcome it - I cherish it -

I would like to invite the student body - that will eventually meet the requirements - to have their own commencement day - in future years to come - to share in this moment - as you look on in wonderment - asking yourself - "will that day ever come?" - I assure you it will - be patient - enjoy your trip - for one day - you will look back - at this whole period of time - and realize - how short it was -

I would like to invite the faculty - from the art instructor - to the math teacher - from English - to music - to science - to history - to language - to the librarian - whose labor - delicate and most arduous task - of teaching these young men - has come to an end today - your patience - your love - your caring - your compassion - your tolerance - your unlimited framework - for your abilities - to teach young minds - and prepare them for life itself - must be commended - there are apprehensions somewhat - as I speak - a little sadness also - to see these young men - leave your ward - I believe it is outweighed - by the tremendous feeling of joy - each of you - also - must feel - by the communion of accomplishment - success - that is witnessed here - today - these young men will never forget you - you have given them life's greatest commodity - knowledge - preparing them to walk life's path - to see the pitfalls - to utilize - to the utmost of their abilities - the teachings - that have been taught here - at this academy - dear faculty - please share in this moment -

to the athletic director - to the coaches - to the assistants - to the program itself - of physical education - the evening - is drawing near - your job - also - has come to an end - you have trained the mind – and body - to act as one - the spirit of winning - eased the heartbreak - when you lost - they have learned what competition - was all about - and sportsmanship - above all - in today's sports oriented society of ours - we do need leaders - you have done - your very best - to uphold the integrity - and dignity - of the task at hand - you have taught these young men - the boundaries of the game - the uncalled for fouls - the timely - time-outs - that they will utilize - for the rest of their life - as they step onto the playing field - of our complex - and ever so changing world - I invite you to share in this moment -

to the parents - let me not forget you - for each of you were present - at the beginning - of their journey - reflect with me - your tears of joy - when your son was born - the days - the years - that followed - when he first smiled - realizing he had a mother and a father - when he took his first step - when he said his first word - when he blew out candle - number 1 - the nights you stayed awake - because he was crying - the fears - that you gently eased - the worries - you endured - for the values you instilled in him - so that he may walk in peace - the times he was sick - and you nursed him back to health - for the love - tears - joys - and understanding - you gave - to accompany him - for his lifetime - the sacrifices - there were so many - the braces on his teeth - the events you came to see your son excel in - how proud you were - and that first time he came to you - and asked you for the car - and the deep concern - each of you have - that your son be a light of hope - for someone whose courage - is faltering - that he may be used as an instrument - to give - to heal - to fulfill life's forum - for the betterment - of mankind - I invite you to share in this moment -

to all the friends - the sisters - the brothers - grandmothers and grandfathers - uncles - aunts and cousins - I invite you to share in this moment - for each of you - share in part - the library of knowledge - that exists in the mind - and heart - of each young man - that is graduating today -

The Alumni Association with its vast outreach program - undertaking the task of linking 65 or 70 years of graduates - to present day functions - at the Academy - which you the class of 1997 - will be a part of - in a very short time - to make the same journey - that many of us have made - I invite you to share in this moment -

The Board of Trustees - year after year - working tirelessly - for the betterment of the school - and the integrity - of the students - making decisions that must be made - for the future of the Academy - to keep up with change - the one facet of life - that is constant - it is not an easy task - I commend each of you - you are truly unsung heroes - I invite you to share in this moment - and to the surrounding staff that support the Academy - the web of intricacies - the secretaries - the staff at the buttery - and the Academy Store - to the gentleman that warms your school in winter - and keeps it clean - by day -

the cornerstone of this Academy - has been laid some 184 years ago -1813 to be exact - The Albany Academy - highest standards - compelling values - the workings of this institution - are far reaching - and never ending - encompassing - and weathering - incredulous - and most phenomenal - periods of history - our Country has faced - from the war of 1812 - the Civil War - the turn of the 20th century - vaccines wiping out small pox - and polio - from the horse - to the car - to the plane - to the rocket - from a walk down Main Street USA - to that historical walk - on the moon itself - we have fought two World Wars - Korea - Vietnam - the Gulf War - heart transplants - are no longer a figment - of the imagination - we have endured earthquakes - hurricanes - tornadoes - floods - snowstorms - heat waves - and the introduction of the atomic age - I could go on but I think I'd better stop here - this is what the Albany Academy has seen - and much more -

today it sees the class of 1997 - standing ever so proud - standing tall - this class will always be unique - to this year - to this day - for you are the only ones graduating - from the Albany Academy - at this particular moment -

today we entrust the present - future - and the overwhelming task - of preserving the ethics - our founders laid for us - to Head of School - Lawrence T. Piatelli - the legacy is in good hands - strong hands - steeped deep in integrity - he dignifies the essence of purity - has compassion - for the soul - he does not compromise - his values - nor justify - his positions -the welfare of the student - is paramount - he will lead most - of this student body - into the 21st Century - he will be able to guide - give you courage - in troubled times - when they arise - he will placate - the fears - encourage - the spirit - he will be your Head of School - he will be your strength - until you have your own - and many a times - he must stand alone - in the solitude of his own thoughts - to make a decision - a very lonely place to be - Head of School - Mr. Piatelli - I invite you to share - in this moment -

to these beautiful young men - I care about you - I care about your welfare - I care that each of you - hear something I say - something that you can carry from me - for the rest of your life - as I will carry this moment - I spend with you - for the rest of my life -

this is truly your moment - this class has spent the better part of six years - together - some more - you know each other very well - you know who did what - when - and where - went on your first dates together - saw your best friend cry - because he broke up with his first girlfriend - went to your first dance together - got your first awards - played your first game of varsity football - swam your first meet - how your heart beat before the start - alliance - and allegiance - you all had with each other - for each other - how about all the worries of passing a test - or getting a paper in on time - or how about when you got in trouble - and were sent to the office - that heart beat again - didn't it? each of you know this school - inside and out - it will never leave you - as long as you live - and somehow I believe -

that these halls - these classrooms - still house some of the teachers - and students - that have passed on -

the step out - the excitement of tomorrow - the accomplishments of today - the journey - with it's twists - some good - some not so good - the joys that will come your way - the girlfriend - that you will marry - the wife - that will bear your child - some of you will be lawyers - doctors - physicists - chemists - actors - businessmen - or just a man - that has a feel - for humanity - you name it - it is here - in this class of 1997 - the journey you're on - will see the blinds open - to the 21st century - it is your century - a lot different from the beginning of the 20th century - for our world - and the people in it - move rapidly - swiftly - and sometimes without thinking - some of you will be asked to solve - world problems - to contribute - to the salvation - of our society itself -

we have a troubled society - beware - some of you here today - may be able to ease the pain - that will exist - in the heart - of the unborn - you are prepared - you are equipped - the shadows that exist for the 21st century - are many - the challenges - that you will be asked to face - in the century to come - are many - from overpopulation - global warming - extinction of our beautiful animals - that inhabit our earth - the pollution - of our oceans - and water ways - the very air - that we breathe - and as the years pass - you will have instant recall - of how it was in the year of 1997 - when you come back to your reunion - you will reflect - for just a moment - relive the picture - that is here today - coupling it with the thought - of how simple life was - in 1997 - for this year truly - belongs to you -

as most of you know - I was here in April - to receive the Distinguished Alumni Award - a tremendous honor - as I sat in the fourth grade room - I thought back to 1943 - my fourth grade teacher - Ms. Swantee - I was sent here - because I couldn't read - or spell - I had been held back 2 years - as I went into this grade - I was not too literate - a mild absence of knowledge - I was 10 years old - when I arrived at the Albany Academy - but before then - I spent three years in an orphanage - from 4 to 7 - not a nice place to be in - in 1937 -

when one tried to run away - they caught him - laid him out on a table - sat us all around - in a big room - made us watch - as they whipped - that boy fiercely - far beyond his crime - I can still see it - I can still hear the cries - by the time I was 7 years of age - the only inner feeling I knew - was loneliness - it haunted me - it beguiled me - it wounded me so deep - that to this day - I can still recall - those feelings - many a time during those years - I huddled in a corner - and cried - those feelings have never left me -

from that orphanage in New York - to another - across the river in Troy - but this time I was close to Albany - I planned an escape - for I knew - where my grandfather lived -

on that Saturday - so many years ago - I - in the literal sense - ran to the house - on the corner - of Maine and New Scotland Avenue - I remember it so clearly - down the stairs - to the cellar - I went - weeping so - most frightened - I pounded on the door - my grandfather came - opened it - I looked up at him and I said - "please don't let them take me back, grandpa" I pleaded - I begged - I cried - he stood six feet two - he picked me up in his arms - and said - "nobody is ever going to take you away again"- I can still feel the strength - the power - of his arms around me - I lived with him - in the cellar - for three glorious years - I never wanted to leave his side - I loved him so much - he gave me hope - he gave me love - he gave me warmth - he gave me compassion - he gave me life - today he is with me - as I walk in the September of my years - the vision of my grandfather - becomes ever so prevalent - for I know he will be - waiting for me - one more time - to hold me - and guide me - through eternity -

I was allowed to have wine - as a youngster - little did I know the effect - it would have on me later -

I want to speak of some of these ironies of life - I don't want to hide behind any mask - of self deluded ideas - or images - I want you young men - to see me as I am - to feel me - to know me - I don't want any of you to think - I'm misleading you - or trying to put something - in your head - that doesn't belong there - I'm not - I do not want - in any way - to tamper - with the inner beauty - each of you have - I am passionately concerned - about each of you - I would love nothing more - than to transmit the passion - that is swirling around - inside of me - to each of you -

so many times you will hear said - "the young men of today - are the hope - and future - of tomorrow" - what a burden - the future of tomorrow - on your shoulders - you haven't gotten through today yet - you will wake up one day - and say - " I am so far behind - it doesn't matter any more " - you are not the hope of the future - you are the hope - you are the young men - of today - the now - each of you have the capability - within your grasp - of making a difference - today - with your knowledge - your energy - your ideas - with your compassion - your tolerance - your understanding - your love - your lust - for life itself - each of you - here today - have that capacity - what a triumph - what a concept -

as I stated - a few moments ago - I was 10 years of age - when I arrived here - at the Academy - I graduated in 1952 - I had a lust for life - the only formal education I received - was here - at this institution - my foundation - I carried this foundation - with me - to New York - to become an actor - the Marine Corp interrupted my quest - for a period of three years - In 1957 I was back acting again - plays in New York - Summer Stock - Repertory - TV - etc. - that little bit of wine - I had as a child - had progressed - as part of my demeanor -

in those late 50's - my talent as an actor grew - at one time Helen Hayes - one of the finest actresses of our time - came back stage - to congratulate me on my performance - Just 7 or 8 years later - in 1966 - after coming to Hollywood - doing many TV shows - in the early sixties - I stood outside 20th Century Fox Studio - I did not know what show - I was on - let alone my lines - I had to ask the guard at the gate - what show I was doing - the use and abuse of alcohol - had rendered me - almost immobile - that talented young actor - the one that could learn 450 lines - and perform three days later - was no more -

for the next three years - the tortures of life - the downhill slide that seemed to never end - the Skid Rows I have seen many - been on many - from New York - to Miami - to Los Angeles - the hopelessness - the fears - the deterioration - of my mind - my body - my soul itself - loneliness - and despair - prevailed - by 1969 I was bleeding internally - huge sores on my body - that would never heal - long hair - bearded - dirty - audio - and visual - hallucinations - black outs - I shuffled as I walked - I spoke in circles - I could not pronounce words - I weighed but 140 pounds - one ounce of alcohol - rendered me immobile - I was 36 years of age - I was dying -

sometime in July of 1969 - a warm - and all encompassing feeling - came over me - the realization that death - was imminent - and near - a moment later - I held a bottle of gin in my hand - and I uttered these words - "please God help me - I don't want to drink this." - next month - July- 28 years will have passed - since my cry - of despair - was heard - for I have been without alcohol or drugs — what so ever in my body - for this period of time - a miracle - for many years - I was ashamed to come back to the Academy - for I had done nothing - accomplished nothing - I just gave heartache - to any one - I came in contact with - I was ashamed - to see my teachers - I was ashamed - to see my classmates - but those same classmates - that were at this ceremony - with me - 45 years ago - came to my side - with love - understanding - they didn't care - what I had accomplished in life - they just wanted to see me - this is the bond - that will last the ages - for each of you - you will all go your separate ways - but the graduating class - of 1997 - from the Albany Academy - will forever - be together - faces will change with time - bodies altered by age - hair thinner- voices differ - but 1997 - will never change - it is here now - and it belongs to you -

in 1987 I was most discouraged - I had done many T.V. shows - worked with some of the top people in Hollywood - honed my talent back - to where it was - when I was a young actor - but disappointment set in - the loss of a Broadway play - the never ending roles on

TV - that were always the same - another realization - that things would never change - came to me - I decided to leave Hollywood - my life as I knew it - I took off in my white truck - for parts unknown - living out of the back of my truck - I traveled absolutely nowhere - for several months - pounding my dashboard - pleading for guidance - begging for help - crying at times - despondent - angry - ever so lonely - one more time - I was 54 years of age.

I'd like to say right here - I had a vision - but that's not true - it sure would make a nice story -

one day while driving in that truck of mine - I had a feeling come over me - to go back to Los Angeles - much against my will I did - as the next several days unfolded - I was directed by this inner feeling - to serve food in the downtown area - known as the Skid Row section - this was not on my personal agenda - I want this understood - but I was obedient - to the feeling -

on December 5 1987 it was a rainy Friday night - cold - miserable - at three in the morning - I made 111 peanut butter and jelly sandwiches - and waited for dawn - a couple of friends of mine - showed up around 8 am - and downtown I went - since that rainy Saturday morning - what was only to be - a short moment in my life - turned into a decade - the 111 sandwiches - have now grown to over 575,000 meals served - to the destitute - the homeless - the downtrodden - the despaired - to the unwanted - and discarded human beings - of our society - where water - is a premium - on hot summer days - soup - a welcome - on cold - winter nights -

in 1992 - I received a magnificent letter - from President Bush - in 1994 a beautiful letter - from President Clinton - and on a warm spring day - in 1995 - over the loud speaker - came these words - "ladies and gentleman - the President of the United States of America " - for one brief moment - as the President came through the Oval Office - into the Rose Garden - the vision of past Presidents became prominent - I saw President Roosevelt - I saw Truman - Eisenhower - I saw President Kennedy - fragmented seconds they were - I realized where I was - I came from my own depths of despair - to the highest office - of our Country - to meet the most powerful man - in the world - and when President Clinton - gave me this elegant medal - he said to me - "thank you Ray - for taking care of the people - of Skid Row - in Los Angeles" - I said thank you Mr. President - I had tears - emotions - wonderment for this precious moment - I accepted this tribute - on behalf of the hundreds of volunteers - the thousands of people that have supported me - and the residents of Skid Row - I am truly interwoven - with this society of people - how proud they were - that I met the President -

I have spent the better part of 10 years of my life - on the streets of Skid Row - this time no alcohol - no drugs - the darkened streets - at night with the fires - the scarred souls - where hope is at a minimum - where rape - murder - prostitution - stabbings - gun shot wounds - drugs - alcohol - gang bangers - violence beyond reproach - sleep by day - somewhat - I have held twisting bodies - ravaged by alcohol convulsions - I have held bodies fallen - by heart attacks - I have held these bodies in my arms - waiting for the paramedics to come - I have hugged the lonely - of our society - I have had them weep - in my arms - I have felt the stomach - of the pregnant women - for they did not know - who the father was - I have intervened in knife fights - I can speak the language of the streets - but also - the language of the heart - I have been the father - mother - sister - brother these people didn't have - every time I left downtown - I also wept - for I realized I was used again - as an instrument - of the Will of God - for the betterment - of mankind - what a privilege - what an honor -

four principles - have dominated my make-up - for many years now - allow me to share them with you - purity - honesty - unselfishness - love - with these principles - and only these principles - I have been able to face - with dignity - the onslaught of humanity that suffers so - I have gained the respect - the love of thousands - I see no color - I see no man nor woman - I only see equality for the human race - there is no room in my heart - for prejudice -

purity - cannot embrace segregation - nor bigotry - nor can it differentiate between male or female - young or old - black or white - one glass of distilled water - one drop of ink - into that glass - it becomes contaminated - deceit - hate - dishonesty - selfishness - resentment - anger - etc. - etc. - become contaminants - of the mind - and soul - when allowed to infiltrate - one's thinking -

the second of these principles is - honesty - most powerful - every moment of life that passes - is a true moment - it is an honest moment or a dishonest moment - you make that choice - each of you are gifted - with the power of choice - within your own framework - you all know the boundaries - of honesty - or dishonesty -

third principle - struggling to stay alive - in our world today - unselfishness - to give purely - to ask for nothing - to put the welfare of someone - or something ahead of oneself - to wake up in the morning - with the sole purpose - of helping mankind - to go to bed at night - knowing I have been a contributor - to the mainstream of life - for the betterment of the human race - to be free of self - with this principle in place - an individual can do - so much - for so many - unselfishness - a priceless principle - attribute - to encompass -

"grant me - that I may not so much seek - to be consoled - as to console - to be understood - as to understand - to be loved - as to love - for it is in the giving - that we receive - it is in the pardoning - that we are pardoned - and it is in dying - that we are born to eternal life" - most succinct - most elegant - most profound - St. Francis of Assisi - 1182-1226

love - is the last of these four principles - in order for me to love - there must be no conditions - a mountain can be moved with this simple concept in place - I received a letter in 1965 - the letter came from my father's brother - I didn't know my father - so obviously - I didn't know his brother - when I opened the letter - a small group of baby pictures - became visible - I looked at the pictures - they were of me - the letter went something like this - on February 18, 1965 - your father - was so riddled with cancer - so weak - he could not hold a glass of water in his hand - nonetheless - he managed - to get out of bed - go over to his dresser - pull out these pictures and say - "this is my son's birthday" - he died 12 days later - he was my father - he loved me - he had no conditions -

I do not rationalize - justify - or compromise these principles - when times are tough - these principles will supersede - the agony - when times are good - they will accent - the joys - you will realize a freedom - beyond any expectation - you will enjoy peace of mind - and you will have power - that will carry you through life's - triumphs - and tragedies - you will be able to function on any plane - of life itself - cope with any situation - that may come up - you will be able to face - any human being - on this earth of ours - with the utmost clarity - and dignity -

you have been educated to the highest level - thus far - you are qualified to enter any college - in the United States - or other parts of the world - what an accomplishment - each of you must be proud - knowing what you have done - a big sigh of relief - also- to realize - that 1997 - has finally come - this is the last time you will be together - in this form - only your memory - will prevail -

I ask each and every person - sitting here today - experiencing this graduation - to focus - for a moment - to channel your love - your compassion - your understanding - your wisdom - your energy - allow it to flow here - to each - and every one - of these beautiful young men - let them take a part of you - with them - now - as they go from here - I ask you - be a part of their journey - be a part of their life - be a part of their world - from this day forward -

there is an adage - It goes like this - "what he is - speaks so loud - I cannot hear a word he says - by example" - each of you - are an example - for the betterment of mankind - not through words - but by action - we are together - we are equal - you are my examples - you are my teachers - I walk - not in front of you - but by your side - whatever it is you must learn in life - always remember - when the pupil is ready - the teacher will appear -

as you walk from these halls - may your hearts be full - may your joys of tomorrow - be your realities of today - each of you are perfect the way you are - I am not out to change anyone - my only challenge in life is to comfort the soul - to still the racing mind - for a moment - to give back to humanity - the courage - it has given me - to carry on - to be an example - of caring - interwoven on the broad cloth of life - are many distractions - pulling and tugging - at the very core - of the ethics - you live by - do not lose sight - of what it is you are destined - to achieve in your lifetime - follow your dreams - stay focused - whether it be selling flowers on the street corner - or re-arranging the stars in the heavens -

falter not as you go - you are well prepared - schooled to the highest level - uncompromised in your thinking - the courage each of you have - will stand strong - you are a most beautiful group - highly gifted - you have given to me - a most precious moment - a moment I will take with me - and share with the people - by the fires - on the streets - of Skid Row - on those cold winter nights - a moment that will last eternally - in my heart - and that lonely - empty feeling inside my soul - that I have carried so long - will be at rest - a bit - when I think of this moment - I walk away from this most magnificent - and beautiful - and energized area - of love - with a lifetime of dreams fulfilled - thank you for allowing me to share - this time - with you -

may each of you - stand tall - among the giants - of humanity - and when you reach your destination - as I have reached mine - I hope you find - what I have found - that the end - was but a beginning - may God bless you - until we meet again -

Head of School - Mr. Piatelli - it is my honor - to present to you - the graduating class of 1997 –

Printed in the United States
131272LV00004BB/1/P

9 781598 588316